During World War 2 thousands of
allied aircrew died whilst training,
some without ever going into action
against the enemy, but whose
sacrifice is often forgotten.

It is to those men that this book
is dedicated.

Contents

Introduction

When *Down in Wales* was published in June 1994, I had no intention of writing another book on the subject but such was the interest from aviation enthusiasts that I was soon striding out once more into the hills.

Since then some of the original sites mentioned have even smaller amounts of wreckage, which is sad. It could be said that I am encouraging its removal by writing these books, despite the fact that I advocate taking photographs rather than wreckage. People are bound to remove some small fragment or two and, at some sites, there will soon come a time when there is nothing left at all. This is doubly unfortunate, not just for the actual remains, but for the fact that accurately finding a site where there is no physical evidence is difficult and often impossible.

There are those in aviation archaeological circles who would like to keep all these sites secret, condemning those who find them and remove small items as "cowboys". (After, of course, going to them themselves and taking the most "interesting" pieces away.) Most of the items removed are, ostensibly, for museums. Most larger museums that have such artefacts, however, no longer exhibit them. They only have so much space and the average visitor would much rather see a whole aeroplane than some twisted metal.

I think that, for future generations, it is important that the exact position of these sites is recorded now, whilst some evidence remains.

(If you are interested in the Battle of Hastings, for instance, you can go to the site, the exact location having been well recorded, even though you would be very lucky to pick up any remains of that encounter.)

I have included, in this book, very few sites where absolutely nothing has been found and then only when I can locate an eye-witness, or one who went to the actual site at the time. You can be sure that the map references are as accurate as I can make them, taking into account that I am only using the same degree of skill in map-reading as the average walker.

As the size and amount of wreckage to be seen can be quite small, I have endeavoured to describe the aircraft, its performance and characteristics as fully as I can. The searcher can, I hope, at least begin to visualise in his minds eye the aircraft which now lies beneath his feet as just a few nuts and bolts and corroded pieces of aluminium.

1996   *T.R. Hill*

Notes on Site Finding

After 50 years or so, we can no longer expect to find large amounts of wreckage but, as explained in volume 1 of *Down in Wales*, this is of no great consequence.

As long as *something* is found, some small pieces of metal, screws, rivets and perspex etc. which can be recognised as parts of an aircraft, the site of the crash will have been located and that, after all, is the object of the exercise.

This, however, does bring its own problems: large wreckage can usually be seen from afar, whereas a dark patch of earth with small fragments is easily missed. Indeed, I have walked within yards of a site and failed to see it. It follows, therefore, that careful pre-planning, with the appropriate map, and measuring off the exact map reference with a ruler, is essential. Make a note of topographical features that will be of assistance in pinpointing the position. Cairns, (although not all are marked on 1¼" OS Maps) a distant TV mast, the shape of a wood and the direction of tracks etc. are all useful aids, but, of course, if the map reference is incorrect there is little that can be done about it. The M.R.s in this book, unlike some others which have been passed on, becoming garbled in the process, have all been checked by me personally. Even so, a certain amount of latitude (so to speak!) must be allowed. I don't have a satellite navigation system and it is notoriously difficult to pinpoint a specific position, especially on high moorland which has no prominent features.

Many sites are on, or across, private property and it is essential to gain the permission of the owner before proceeding. This is not as difficult as it might seem. Look on the map for the nearest farm and if the land does not belong to them, they surely know who does own it.

As in the previous volume, a few post-war crashes have been included. The mist shrouded hill of Wales together with pilot error and aircraft malfunction can still exert a heavy toll.

Searching in Safety

None of the sites included in this book involve the slightest mountaineering skill. Indeed, the author, despite many thousands of flying hours behind him, (including many on trials work, standing in the open rear end of a Blackburn Beverley (of revered memory) the ground flashing by a mere three yards beneath his feet) views climbing more than half a dozen steps up a ladder with some apprehension.

On the other hand, you are unlikely to encounter a lady with handbag and high heels at any of them; in other words, most involve a good, stiff walk, generally uphill.

Take warmer clothing than you think you will need; the temperature reduces by about 3°F for each 1000 feet above sea level and on higher ground the wind-chill factor will be more pronounced. Take food, compass and, if in the hills, let someone know where you are going.

Remember, even if you don't find the site, you will go into some of the most beautiful country side in Wales.

Aircraft Wreckage

The ownership of the remains of British, United States and German aircraft is vested in the Ministry of Defence.

Permission of that Ministry should be sought if it is intended to recover any parts found. This is mainly intended for groups who wish to actually excavate the site, and not really aimed at someone casually picking up a small item, however, technically, no part should be removed. This may seem a trifle ridiculous when it is known that groups, local councils, individuals etc., have been carting away wreckage wholesale for years, and in some cases, selling it.

Really, it is best not to remove parts but to photograph them for later identification — this will also have the advantage of leaving something for successive generations to find.

The contact address for those who wish to recover items is:

MINISTRY OF DEFENCE
ROOM F63
BUILDING 255
RAF INNSWORTH
GLOUCESTER
GL3 1EZ

Maps

All references given in this book are for Ordnance Survey Landranger 1:500,000 series 1¼ inches to the mile, although often, Outdoor Leisure maps 1:25,000 series will prove useful.

The Country Code

Respect the life and work of the countryside.
Guard against all risk of fire.
Leave gates as you find them.
Keep dogs under control.
Keep to public paths across farmland.
Take your litter home.
Protect wildlife, plants and trees.
Take care on country roads.
Help keep water clean.
Don't damage trees, hedges and walls.

Junkers Ju88 of 3(F) Aufkl. Gr.123

September 7th, 1940. The third and most critical phase of the Battle of Britain, where the Luftwaffe attacked RAF airfields, had just ended. A new phase of attacks on London was about to begin. The code word "Cromwell" had been issued to the Army to bring them to the highest state of readiness for invasion.

During the previous week, however, other cities such as Liverpool had received the attention of the German bombers. (Indeed, during the period of the Battle of Britain 1,957 tons of bombs were dropped on Merseyside.)

The German High Command were anxious to know what their bombing had achieved and the reconnaissance group of Luftflotte 2 (Airfleet 2), 3 (F) Aufkl. Gr.123*, based at Buc near Paris, were given the task of photographing the area. They were equipped with the Junkers Ju88, an efficient twin-engined bomber but in this case carrying a number of cameras.

The crew detailed for the task consisted of:

LEUTNANT ERICH BOHLE (Pilot and ex Cambridge student).
OBERLEUTNANT HANS KAUTER (Aircraft commander).
UNTEROFFIZIER GOTHARD LEISLER (Gunner)
UNTEROFFIZIER WALTER KOBOLD (Gunner)

One of these was also the Navigator.

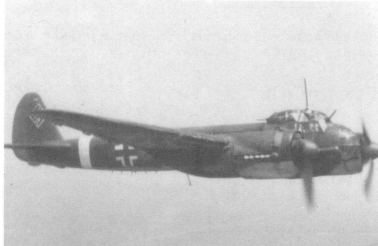

A Junkers Ju88

Ob. Lt. Hans Kauter.
His epaulettes and lapel insignia seem to be that of a Hauptmann, which is the next higher rank, equivalent to a Flight Lieutenant.
On his right breast is the standard Luftwaffe eagle, whilst on his left is his pilot's wings and Iron Cross, first class.

* Approximates to 3rd squadron of 123 photographic reconnaissance group.

Ob. Lt. Kauter, however, was no ordinary aircraft commander. He was a photo. intelligence officer from the Luftwaffe Test Centre at Rechlin.

At 0930 on September 7th they took-off; their mission to photograph bomb damage in Liverpool and Crewe.

At 20,000 feet, their progress went unremarked; during that day over a thousand German aircraft crossed the English coast. They were over Hoylake, on the Wirral peninsula, when the local Observer Corps unit reported an unidentified aircraft overhead.

The scene now shifts to RAF Hawarden near Chester, home, at this time, to No.7 OTU. This unit was fully occupied training replacement Spitfire pilots, many of whom had only half a dozen hours on type before being thrown into the conflict.

Sgt L.S. Pilkington, an instructor (late of No. 73 squadron) flying R6924, one of the early cannon armed Spitfires was accompanied by a young Sergeant pilot in another Spitfire, for formation flying practice, when he was instructed to climb to 20,000 feet to investigate an unidentified aircraft. Instructing his pupil to return to base he opened the throttle to maximum climbing power.

Two other Spitfires from the OTU now joined him: Sgt Payne, a fellow instructor and the acting C.O. Wg. Cdr. Ira Jones, DSO, MC, DFC, MM a veteran of the 1914-1918 war. As they drew closer, the aircraft was identified as a Ju88.

The C.O. expended all his ammunition with no obvious effect and left the two Sergeants to continue the chase. The rear gunner of the Ju88 kept up a stream of accurate fire, damaging both wings of Sgt Pilkington's aircraft, whilst Lt Bohle threw his aircraft into violent evasive manoeuvres.

By now the chase had taken the combatants over North Wales. Sgt Pilkington gave the Ju88 a burst of fire from about 450 yards, but the port cannon jammed after only three rounds had been fired. (This was a common occurrence on early cannon equipped Spitfires, which were little used by front line squadrons during the Battle because of this and was the reason why they were being used by the OTU.) *(See note at end of chapter.)

Sgt Pilkington then closed in to about 75 yards and opened fire with his sole remaining cannon. Shells striking its port engine and with glycol coolant streaming behind, the Ju88 entered cloud.

The Spitfires returned to Hawarden, leaving Lt Bohle with the unenviable task of trying to climb, with one engine out of action, over the hills leading up to Aran Fawddwy.

This was clearly impossible and with great skill and an equal amount of luck, he put the aircraft down, at an angle of about 40 degrees, on the western slopes of Drum Ddu. There was no fire and the aircraft was relatively undamaged; all the crew members, however, had injuries of varying severity. Being the least injured, Ob. Lt. Kauter, with a few broken ribs, cuts and bruises set off, after first destroying the various secret documents he was carrying.

Seeing the river below, (Afon Clywedog), he decided to follow it down, reasoning that there would be some sort of dwelling nearby.

It turned out to be a long, rough walk of about 2.5 miles, during which he took his service pistol to pieces and threw them into the river; being armed would have served no purpose in his present predicament. (The pieces of this weapon have never been recovered.)

At last he reached the farmhouse of Gelli Ddolen and knocked on the door. One can imagine the distress he was in but his condition could not have appeared too menacing as Mrs Jane Jones, the farmer's wife, let him in.

She sat him by the fire and in halting English, he told her what had happened. Whilst he sipped a cup of tea, she ran out to her husband, Idwal, working in the meadow. He set off at once to nearby Mallwyd and, using the telephone in the Post Office, informed the authorities in Machynlleth, some eleven miles away.

Before the army guard party arrived at the scene some hours elapsed. Meanwhile a number of local people had gone up to view the wreckage and, using five-barred gates lifted off their hinges as stretchers, they brought down the rest of the injured crew. Together with Ob. Lt. Kauter, they were taken on a trailer to hospital in Machynlleth.

Later, guided by farm workers, the guard party set off up the hillside, not following the river but taking a shorter route to the east.

By the time they reached the crash site the mist had come down enveloping the hillside, which prevented their relief until the next day.

September 8th, 1940. RAF personnel are removing equipment,
whilst the guard party sit nearby.

September 1994. Hafotty-Lluest-Badlon can be seen clearly in the centre of the photograph.
In the top photograph taken in 1940 it can be seen at top right.

Whilst this was going on, an RAF party, keen to investigate the wreckage, arrived at Gelli Ddolen but were unable to go up until the mist lifted on the following day.

A minute investigation of the aircraft was made. This was a necessary practice carried out by both sides during the war, in order to keep abreast of any new developments.

After all special equipment had been removed, the salvage party arrived and took away the remaining wreckage.

A wing of the Ju88 was taken back to RAF Hawarden, as a war trophy.

The first crash of a German aircraft on Welsh soil was over and silence once more descended on these

Gelli Ddolen, home of Idwal and Jane Jones in 1940.

Hans Kauter sat here, by the fireplace, on September 7th, 1940.

desolate hills, leaving them to the sheep and those who tended them.

The crew of the Ju88 were eventually transported to a Prisoner of War camp in Canada. Many POW's especially those thought likely to attempt escape, were sent across the Atlantic in ships returning empty after bringing in much needed supplies. More amenable prisoners, especially the Italians, stayed in the UK, many of them working happily on farms in Mid-Wales.

★ ★ ★

In June 1985 the highlight of the year for the now defunct Machynlleth Aircraft Discoverers was the visit of Hans Kauter to Wales. They took him first to Machynlleth hospital, where he was able to show his wife, Margret, where he had been nursed.

Then they went to Mallwyd, home now of Idwal and Jane Jones. The event was celebrated by the eating of damson jam sandwiches, in memory of the day, 45 years earlier, when Hans Kauter knocked on the door of Gelli Ddolen whilst Mrs Jones was making damson jam.

The party then visited Gelli Ddolen farmhouse which has now fallen into disrepair.

The MAD group members included Bill Breeze the only living survivor of the crash of Wellington R1286.

Both Bill and Idwal have since passed away.

A number of interesting points arise in connection with this crash.

The Spitfire of Sgt Pilkington is described in other publications as R6942. Perusal of the definitive book on the Spitfire* shows that no such serial was issued. R6924 was indeed a Spitfire and was on the strength of 7 OTU at the time, so I think it is pretty safe to assume that this was the aircraft involved.

Another book states that the Ju88 pilot, Lt Bohle, was the one who followed the river down the mountain but I think that, as we have the evidence of Hans Kauter himself, this will have to be dismissed.

Another story that has gone the rounds for many years since the time of the crash, is that one of the crew members was a Gestapo officer. The Ju88 had a crew of four and Hans Kauter is adamant that no such officer was on board.

The story probably came about because of an incident described by Idwal Jones. Whilst the casualties were being carried down the mountain, one of them ripped of his insignia and threw it to the ground saying, " . . . Next time we will be fighting together". (This, doubtless refers to the fact that Hitler had hopes of Britain and Germany joining together against Communism.) This gesture, however, might have been seen by some to be the action of a Gestapo man trying to cast aside his SS emblems in order to appear as an ordinary airman.

Hans Kauter, as related, was certainly still with us in 1985, as I hope he remains today, but what of the others? According to Kauter, one went into East Germany and has not been heard of since. Another became a dentist in Caracas, Venezuela; a bolt-hole for many Nazis.

Whilst in POW camp in Canada, Kauter was in the same hut as Von Werra the only German POW to escape and return to Germany. He was subsequently killed later in the war, and his story was related in the film "The One That Got Away".

Lest too much sympathy for the German crew be generated by the foregoing story, it must be said, that according to eye witnesses, they were Nazis of the most arrogant type.

A final little tit-bit of local heresay. Before the guard arrived on the scene, one of the people to go up to the site was a local parson. From the wreckage he removed one of the cameras and took it home. Later, hearing that the recovery team were searching for this missing piece of equipment he had misgivings. Unable to get close to the aircraft, he dumped the offending article in a nearby stream, where it was eventually found by the search party.

★ ★ ★

Notes

The Ju88 came from Aufklaerungsgruppe 123, one of three reconnaissance formations in Luftflotte 2 (Airfleet 2) based in France and Belgium. The aircraft was one of 71 serviceable aircraft available at this phase of the Battle of Britain. They were equipped with bomber aircraft and carried full defensive armament, but cameras instead of bombs.

Aufkl Gr.123 had the distinction, in early 1945, of being the first reconnaissance unit of any air arm to be equipped with jet aircraft. Using the twin-engined ARADO 234 they flew a number of sorties over southern England unhindered by the British defences.

British reconnaissance aircraft, with much greater distances to cover over enemy territory, lacked the reassurance of defensive armament which was removed to give extra speed and range.

No. 7 OTU shot down three enemy aircraft during the Battle of Britain; a Heinkel 111 on August 14th and a Dornier 17 on September 18th, which crashed into the sea off Rhyl.

In June 1938, 19 squadron was the first unit to receive the new Spitfire.

In 1939 some 30 Spitfires armed with 20mm Oerlikon cannon were used on an experimental basis, scoring their first victory, a Heinkel He111, on January 13th, 1940. Nineteen squadron received half a dozen of these aircraft, but during the Battle of Britain gun stoppages made them unpopular. The C.O. Sgn Ldr Pinkham, wrote to the AOC suggesting that they be given to an OTU in exchange for the older, machine-gun armed, models.

* Spitfire: The History. Morgan and Shacklady.

His suggestion was accepted and on September 4th, 1940, 19 squadron delivered its cannon armed aircraft to 7 OTU Hawarden (including the one which shot down the Ju88).

According to the 19 squadron diary, the aircraft they received were " . . . what wrecks!" but " . . . at least the guns fire".

★ ★ ★

Before visiting this site it would be worthwhile going to Braich-Llwyd farm at MR 125/909129. The farmer Emyr Jones (son of Idwal mentioned in the foregoing narrative) may well give you permission to go to Gelli Ddolen, now derelict. On going inside you can see the fireplace, next to which Hans Kauter sat, whilst waiting to be taken to hospital.

Mr Jones can also show you the aluminium paddle from the Ju88s dinghy; it hangs from the ceiling of a nearby outhouse.

The site can be reached from Braich-Llwyd as it is not a particularly hard walk, but as most of the hillside is managed by the Nature Conservation who are studying the upland flora and fauna of the region, it would probably be better to approach from the Llanymawddwy direction. A Forestry Commission track runs alongside the river to within a few hundred yards of the crash site.

As it is no longer grazed, the heather on the hillside is thick and deep. A local farmer I spoke to thinks that the heather will swamp any other interesting species of plant that may be there, but that is another story.

This is one site which, without finding any physical evidence of the crash, can still be accurately pin pointed by using the photographs reproduced here.

Below is the Nant Badlon, with the ruins of the old farmhouse Hafotty-Lluest Badlon* on its far side. To the left the river curves sharply northwards; both these features can be seen on the photograph taken on September 8th, 1940 and on that taken exactly 54 years later.

Because of the deep heather it is difficult to search for any fragments that might remain. The aircraft, though relatively undamaged, must have been broken up into quite small pieces in order to remove it. Something must still be there, but finding it is another matter.

MR 125/915163

* This name approximates to 'Summer place on the sheepwalk by the Badlon river'.

Handley-Page Halifax B111 LW366

The story of this crash was told in *Down in Wales* but since then I have, by dint of much research, made contact with the sole living survivor of the disaster. Don James, now living in Canada has given me a first-hand account of the events, which I reproduce in full here.

★ ★ ★

The B Mk III was the culmination of years of trying to get the Halifax right: Drag, caused by inefficient radiators and exhaust stubs, control difficulties, for which the rudders were responsible and a host of other factors meant that its full potential was not realised for some time.

The aircraft loss rate reflects this; the loss rate of the Lancaster was considerably lower than that of the Halifax for tonnage of bombs dropped. The Short Stirling was even less efficient, due mainly to its short wing span of 99 feet. (A figure arrived at solely because it would fit into the standard RAF hangar; but that is another story.) A former bomber pilot told me that most crews were fiercely proud of the aircraft that brought them home in one piece and, in any case, usually had no experience of the 'better' types.

Before the Mark III came along there were about six other marks, and numerous sub series, in the attempt to make it a more efficient machine.

If all this makes it appear that the Halifax was not really worth the effort, it must be remembered that it was the first RAF four engined bomber to enter service. It did sterling work (no pun intended) in Bomber Command, the bravery of its crews off-setting its deficiencies.

Before telling the wireless operator's story, a short resume of the accident is, perhaps, needed.

Halifax LW366 of 420 sqn RCAF took off from its base at Tholthorpe near York at 1340 hours on February 29th, 1944, on a cross-country exercise.

The crew consisted:

F. Sgt	HARDY	Pilot
Sgt	CUNNINGS	Bomb Aimer
Fg. Off.	HEDRICH	Navigator
Sgt	NIXON	Mid-Upper Gunner
Fg. Off.	JAMES	Wireless Op/AG
Sgt	JOHNSON	Rear Gunner
F. Sgt	WILLOUGHBY	Flight Engineer

Let the wireless operator, Don James take it from here:

★ ★ ★

The Wireless Operator's Story

The ill-fated flight took place on February 29th, 1944. My log book (which I fortunately still have), shows the total duration of this flight, from take-off to final end, at only one hour and thirty minutes of air time. Four-twenty Squadron at Tholthorpe was on a stand down from operations, as the weather was too poor over Germany. The bombers on the station had armament and gas* on board for a raid into Germany which was called off. As air command ruled that they could not remain bombed up longer than 24 hours (perhaps it was 48?), the bombs were unloaded and it was decided to mount some navigation flights to keep the air crews in top form. This was the reason that this aircraft had 1600 gallons of 100 octane gas aboard when it crashed.

If the circumstances of this crash left many questions unanswered it was because most of the crew did not survive to recount the details leading up to the final end. I was the wireless operator and was off the

An RCAF Halifax III prepares
to take-off from Tholthorpe.

Don James as an aircrew trainee.

No. 6 Observer's Advanced Flying Unit Staverton, near Cheltenham
on August 21st, 1943. Don James is the tallest on the back row.
Those marked with a 'X' did not survive the war; about 50%.

intercom working with a station, (the name of which I have forgotten because of the long time that has elapsed). Our engineer, Jim Willoughby, was knocked out, as you will learn later and had a rather sketchy recolleciton of details of much of the proceedings.

We were approaching the coast of Wales, expecting to make a landfall in the region of Cross Inn. Suddenly I felt the aircraft take a steep dive to starboard. It rolled over at the bottom of this dive and the G forces showed it was pulling out to make a climb to port. This is a classic manoeuvre, used by bombers at the time, to turn into a fighter's attack. It forces him to make an even tighter turn to bring his guns to bear, as he is, after all, flying a gun platform. He must point his aircraft at the bomber to bring his guns to bear. This is a tactic that you would repeat as required, climbing and diving alternately, turning in the direction of any attack and then making your next move in the opposite direction. This evasive tactic was intended to allow evasive action while maintaining altitude and course; albeit a zig-zag course.

I heard a loud bang right over my head and in this aircraft I was essentially sitting under the pilot, next to the port engine nacelle. (More about this later, when the people from Handley Page came in to question us.) At this point, just as the G forces were at their height, all four engines quit. Switching back onto the intercom, I heard Skeet Hardy the pilot, shout "Abandon aircraft, jump, jump". This was the standard statement for an emergency jump, which means to use the nearest escape hatch. In a non emergency jump, all personnel would come forward, use the front hatch, and be counted to make sure everyone was out.

I was using a trailing aerial for the wireless set that has about two pounds of lead balls on the end of stainless steel wire. This is supposed to be jettisoned before anyone bales out, as it might hit someone in event of this action. It is fastened at the end with cotton twine and the procedure was to leave a few turns of the stainless on the reel and hit the quick release button, so that this cotton line will snap when it runs out. I turned to the left to do this and, at this point, I felt the aircraft must have reached stalling speed. The nose dropped with such swiftness that it threw me against the wireless set, for I had already undone my seat belt. I let the stainless aerial run out and jettison. Then, turning to the right, picked up my chest parachute pack, which was in a container on the floor beside me, and clipped it on.

I stepped to the right, past the set and the curtain between myself and the navigator, (which was blowing frantically around at this time). It was then that I discovered the perspex nose in the aircraft was gone and so were the navigator and the bomb-aimer. Their parachutes were still in the containers on the side of the aircraft and the escape hatch in the floor was still in place. I assumed, when thinking about this later, that the bomb-aimer may have been thrown into the perspex front of the aircraft, when the nose dropped so quickly and the navigator, in trying to save him from falling out, was pulled with him when it broke away.

Trying to open the escape hatch proved to be more than a little difficult. As I remember, it was hinged to rise to the front of the aircraft. (Probably designed that way in order that anyone doing this chore would not be in the way of any person coming down the steps leading the nose of the aircraft.) However, this design feature did not consider the fact that, with the perspex nose gone, the air rushing in as the aircraft was diving kept snapping the hatch closed.

It was at this point that parachute silk filled the front of the aircraft (it was like one was hiding under a bed sheet) and a body fell on top of me. I thought, "this is it, I will not have time to get the hatch open before we hit the ground". However, this situation was momentary, for suddenly the parachute and the body were gone. Later I found out that this was Jim, the Flight Engineer. He had, apparently, hit his face on the oxygen controls, on the front of the dashboard facing the steps and knocked himself out.

Apparently his pilot chute must have got out the front of the airplane and sucked him out like a champagne cork popping. I am still a loss how this could have occurred, with the air rushing in like it did. Perhaps the rushing air formed some kind of vortex, travelling in a circle. However, when he recovered consciousness he was descending on his parachute, as he later recounted to me.

I finally managed to get the hatch open and, turning it kitty-corner in the oblong opening, dropped it out as instructed in our procedures. Through the opening, the ground seemed very close. I bailed out, feet first, facing aft. (I can remember thinking that this was no time for hesitation, with the ground that close.) The aircraft passed over me and I pulled the rip cord. The sudden jolt from the chute opening caused both my flying boots to depart and I was now in my stocking feet. I was in the air a very short time and guessed later that I could not have been much higher than five hundred feet when I got out.

The impact was not hard, somewhat like jumping off the flat car of a train at fifteen miles an hour. Now on my feet I looked to see if I could ascertain where the aircraft had gone. There was a dark cloud of smoke less than a mile away and, gathering up my chute, I headed for a farmhouse that was not too far away. There I encountered the flight engineer, who told me he had come down in water. He was in the company of the farmer himself.

Later he told me that, while procedures about coming down in the water suggest that you wait till your feet touch and then hit the quick release button to prevent the chute from collapsing over you, he had not followed these instructions to the letter. He had estimated that he was within five feet and hit the button at this point. He must have been about twenty-feet up and, as the depth of the water was only waist high, he knifed through it and hit the bottom. He was limping badly when I first saw him. He also told me later that the farmer thought he was a German. At the time we were all wearing flying coveralls over our battle dress and there was no insignia on them. The farmer was carrying a pitch fork and Jim was not inclined to argue with him. This was apparently solved by a boy who told the farmer, "I think he's one of ours." I believe the farmer spoke Welsh, for I had difficulty making myself understood when I asked if he had a pair of rubber boots or something I could use to get to the crash. There was some snow on the ground, and I, of course, was still in my stocking feet. It was the farmer's wife who produced a pair of shoes, about size seven; my own size being twelve I gratefully declined. This all took less than three minutes or so. Dumping my parachute on the floor of the farmhouse, I then took off, cross-country, in the direction of the smoke cloud. Not to be dissuaded because of his feet, Jim insisted on following and, as it was rough going, was soon left some distance back. At that point I was not inclined to wait, in case there was someone I could pull from the crashed aeroplane. This proved to be a forlorn hope for, on reaching the scene, the only thing I could recognise was the rubber dinghy. It had come out of the port wing and was burning furiously. The engines seemed to have dug a long pit that was filled with gasoline and burning in a wall of flame at the time.

Shortly, I was joined by the engineer and two women, who I assumed to be a mother and daughter. They had run over to us from an adjacent farmhouse. I remember they seemed a little hysterical and kept kissing us on the cheek and asking if we were all right. I was told later, although I did not see it, that the tail section had broken off, gone over the farmhouse and set fire to a hay rick on the far side and that the tail gunner was still in his turret. I assume that, with the power gone, his electric-hydraulic system for the turret would not function. In which case he would have had to crank the turret around by hand, (reaching into the aircraft for his chute) and crank it back sideways to bail out backwards from the doors in the turret. I doubt if there had been time for this manoeuvre. I was also advised later that the mid-upper gunner had opened his chute too soon and, wrapping it around the tail plane, had followed the aircraft into the ground. Skeet Hardy, the pilot, was still in the Halifax when it hit. The only good thing about this was that he would feel no pain; it would have been instantaneous.

At this point military vehicles had started to pull up and they insisted that the engineer and I come into the farmhouse, as they had a doctor with them. Where they came from I don't know; some of the uniforms were American, so there must have been a military installation somewhere.

We felt this was unnecessary, as our wounds (if you could call them that), appeared to be superficial. I had a cut in the skull under the hair line, for which someone suggested they should shave my head. I also had the left eyebrow laid open where a buckle on the harness had hit my head when the parachute opened. I managed to convince them that I didn't need my head shaved and they stitched and patched me with what I considered oversize bandages. In Jim's case, his teeth were showing through his upper lip where his face had hit the oxygen controls. This they stitched up and gave him a rig like eyeglasses, which ran back to his ears to support the lip in position. Even small cuts in the head or face area bleed profusely like a nosebleed. I think, from the amount of blood on the front of our flying coveralls, they initially thought we must be in worse condition than we were. Some one who was among those searching the wreck area came in then with some brass buttons and asked if we would know who they belonged to. Jim and I told them that, as everyone was wearing battle dress except the pilot who was wearing his dress tunic, they could be his, as far as identification was concerned. I remember Jim and me looking at each other and he told me later that he felt the same as I did — the realisation that the whole crew was gone — hit for the first time. At this point someone produced some whiskey from somewhere and insisted we both have a drink. Someone else came in and advised us that transportation was waiting to take us to the

The crew of LW366.

F. Sgt Willoughby, the Flight Engineer, and Don James on leave at Leamington Spa after the crash.

nearest RAF base. The doctor pressed a couple of pills in our hands. He advised us to take them before going to sleep (which incidentally neither of us did) and we never saw the crash site again.

The fond memory I have of this whole nasty incident was the courtesy and kindness the Welsh and English people displayed to us on the way from the crash site to our home base. We were, after all, only two of the millions of service men in the British Isles at this time.

The adjutant and an officer from the WAAF (Women's Auxiliary Air Force), at the RAF facility we were taken to (I believe it was near "Fishguard",* and the station was engaged in towing drogues for air firing practice), took us out to the local pub for a drink that night, before retiring. People kept sending free drinks to the table. I don't know whether they had heard of the crash, or saw the bandages we had but it certainly was a nice gesture. I cashed a cheque for I think it was fifteen pounds, at the station, to get money for train fare back to the base and it was never presented to my account.

The station had loose packed our parachutes and, on the journey back, we were carrying these, our parachute harness and our coveralls as baggage. We were also wearing our flying boots. The station had given me a brand new pair, with straps and buckles at the top, so they would not come off in the air! We were without headgear as it had remained in the aircraft. All of this, I guess, made us rather obvious. People, including one woman in her seventies, kept rising on the crowded trains and offering us their seats. We declined as gracefully as we could, feeling a little sheepish about the whole thing.

Jim and I got off in Aberystwyth for the night and, while I cannot remember the name of the Hotel it was closest to the railway station. We were standing in a line that was two or three wide and extended the length of half a block, all of them waiting to check in. We had only been in this line for about three minutes, with all our paraphernalia, when someone from the hotel Management came down the line and ushered us away. He told us not to bother with checking in, "Just give us your names and we will do it for you". They gave us a room with about five beds in it. When they asked if we had eaten and learned we had not, they got the cook out of bed (although we protested) and had him cook up bacon and eggs for us. The room had radiators, which were heated by gas and had a meter to put shillings in to turn it on. They even put two or three shillings in this and would not hear of recompense. I shall never forget all this attention; we began to feel like royalty, albeit a little on the humble side.

* Aberporth

The final chapter in this incident was an enquiry by the people from Handley Page, who came to our station as part of the investigation into the crash. I told them that the loud bang I had heard over my head was the disintegration of the control rods, leading from the pilots steering column to the elevators and rudder on the tail assembly. (An event that would probably cause him to close the throttles on the engines, as he could no longer pull the aircraft out of its dive?) While the engineer could not remember seeing him do this, he concluded it was a logical assumption, for it would be most illogical for our engines to quit at once. I believe they were never able to establish that this was so from the wreckage and listed the cause as unknown.

★　★　★

Don James in 1994.

During the war, the Irvin Air Chute company presented a gold caterpillar badge to all those using their parachutes to save their lives.

LESLIE L. IRVIN
F.R.Ae.S., F.R.S.A.
HONORARY SEC.
EUROPEAN BRANCH

c/o IRVING AIR CHUTE
OF GREAT BRITAIN LTD.
ICKNIELD WAY
LETCHWORTH, HERTS

CATERPILLAR CLUB

August 31, 1944.

F/O. D. A. James, J.26859,
c/o. R.C.A.F. Overseas H.Q.,
20, Lincoln's Inn Fields,
LONDON......W.C.2.

Dear F/O. James,

I am terribly sorry for the delay in sending you your Caterpillar, but it has only just been received.

I have much pleasure in enclosing it herewith, with our complinents and the hope that it brings you Good Luck.

Yours sincerely,

Leslie L. Irvin.

MEL.
Encl. Pin.

A little bit of trivia regarding my own crash: At the Heavy Conversion Unit I was previously posted to, with another crew, we were to be posted out to an operational squadron, when I was put into the hospital with tonsillitis. They had to pick up a substitute wireless operator and he was killed by anti aircraft fire over Hamburg. I recrewed with Harry Skeet Hardy after I got out of the hospital. I often think I had some kind of a guardian angel.

The other bit of trivia: When I got back to Tholthorpe, I turned in my loose packed parachute and they charged me one shilling and sixpence for the D ring on my parachute and sixpence hapenny for the dinghy whistle on my collar, both of which disappeared in the crash. I remember thinking this was pretty stingy treatment, as I didn't ask for the problem and could hardly be expected to hang onto the D ring when I pulled the chute. They said I was issued them from stores and was expected to return them.

MR 146/552641

Vickers Armstrong's Wellington Mk 1c R1491

The Wellington, affectionately known to serviceman and civilians alike as the "Wimpy", bore the brunt of Bomber Command's early night raids on Germany. It was not until October 1943, however, that the Wellington made its last operational flight over Germany; by that time it had dropped over 42,000 tons of bombs on enemy targets. It continued in service with other Commands and some units were still using the training version, the Mark X, some years after the war.

Nearly all aircrew destined for Bomber Command served on an OTU equipped with Wellingtons at some time during their training but, as mentioned in another Chapter, their 2 Bristol Pegasus 1,000 hp radial engines were hard pressed to maintain reasonable progress when the aircraft was fully laden. When an engine failed, especially with a novice crew, the results were often disastrous. Literally hundreds of Wellingtons were lost because of engine failure and how many of those failed to return from operations did so from this and not because of enemy action, will never be known.

Perhaps a little note here of how the crews at Operational Training Units were trained and selected would not come amiss. All aircrew "trades" were trained in their own speciality at flying schools devoted to each particular job. They finally all came together at the OTU and were taught to fly as a team on practice flights. These culminated in an actual raid, usually on a relatively "soft" target, not too far into enemy territory. A number of crews were lost on these raids, never having served on an operational squadron.

The RAF left the crews to select themselves. (A pilot might wander up to a Navigator and enquire if he was flying with anyone. If the answer was "No", he could suggest that they flew together. The rest of the crew was then completed in similar fashion.) By this casual method they were far more likely to work as an efficient team than if they were detailed by the RAF and, of course, they had only themselves to blame if they made a poor choice!

Night cross-country exercises were viewed by most young OTU crews with some trepidation. On one unit five aircraft were lost on cross-countries in a week.

★   ★   ★

On the evening of January 26th 1943 at 15 OTU Harwell, Berkshire, a cross-country exercise was planned. The crew of Wellington R1491 were:

SGT C. EDWARDS	Pilot
SGT L. MUSTON	Navigator
SGT G. OTTLEY	Wireless Operator
SGT B. PARKER	Rear Gunner
SGT J. TODD	Bomb Aimer

Whilst flying over Mid-Wales they were overtaken by some catastrophic event, the true nature of which will never be known. From previous experience, however, an engine fire would be the most likely cause. The aircraft crashed in flames on the minor road between Llansilin and Oswestry. An engine hit the roof of Bwlch-y-Rhiw farmhouse and smashed through the top floor, killing Edwin Williams and his wife Annie. Their 16 year old son Daniel was sleeping in another room. He ran down the back staircase and bravely rescued his 10 year old sister Nancy and a Land girl, by putting up a ladder to their bedroom window. Tragically there was nothing they could do to save their parents, who must have been killed instantly.

When the recovery team finally arrived, the bodies of only two of the crew members could be found, that of the Navigator and the Bomb Aimer. They now rest in the military section of Oswestry cemetery. The other crew members were officially listed as missing.

In January 1993 a commemorative plaque was unveiled on Bwlch-y-Rhiw farmhouse by the Mayor of Oswestry.

★   ★   ★

*Bwlch-y-Rhiw farmhouse
in 1995.*

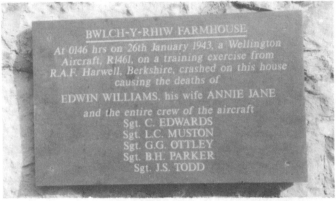

BWLCH-Y-RHIW FARMHOUSE
At 0146 hrs on 26th January 1943, a Wellington
Aircraft, R1461, on a training exercise from
R.A.F. Harwell, Berkshire, crashed on this house
causing the deaths of
EDWIN WILLIAMS, his wife ANNIE JANE
and the entire crew of the aircraft
Sgt. C. EDWARDS
Sgt. L.C. MUSTON
Sgt. G.G. OTTLEY
Sgt. B.H. PARKER
Sgt. J.S. TODD

A 'Wimpy' crew, ready for an "Op".

The present owner of Bwlch-y-Rhiw, Bill Richards, was happy to let me look around the garden, where I found a few small fragments. He also showed me the top of the front door frame where the paint inside still shows signs of singeing.

Just a few hundred yards down the road, I looked in at the house called Lledrod. Taking me into the back garden, the present owner, Mrs A. Sharpe, showed me the tip of a propeller blade, still with its original yellow paint.

I was touched when she told me that she wanted to keep it as a small memorial to those who died on that tragic day.

MR 126/227298

Gloster Gladiators Mk.1 K7927 and K8045

A development of the Gloster Gauntlet, the Gladiator was the last biplane fighter to see service with the RAF. Powered by a Bristol Mercury radial engine of 840 hp, it could attain a speed of 253 mph and had an endurance of some 2 hours. It was armed with four 0.303 inch machine guns: two in the fuselage, firing through the propeller arc and two mounted under the lower wings.

Gladiators were operated by 263 squadron from a frozen lake, in Norway, in 1940 but could not stem the oncoming tide of the Luftwaffe ranged against them. Though no Gladiators were lost in the air, most were destroyed on the ground by German bombing. The surviving pilots were evacuated by the aircraft carrier HMS Glorious, which itself was sunk by the German battle-cruiser Scharnhorst, whilst on its way back to Britain.

The Gladiator is, no doubt, best remembered for its part in the defence of Malta, where, at one phase of the battle, the island's air defence was reduced to just three Gladiators. These soon became known as 'Faith', 'Hope' and 'Charity'. (The skeleton of 'Faith, N5520', is now in the war museum in Valletta, Malta.)

By June 1940, however, Hurricanes and, later, Spitfires arrived to replace them.

* * *

During the war a number of films were made with the full co-operation of the fighting services. Many were produced by various government and military film units.

One hesitates to use the word "propaganda", a term more reminiscent of Herr Göebbels, Hitler's minister responsible for such activities but these films were, nevertheless, meant to raise the morale and uplift the spirits of people in a rather drab war-time Britain.

Gladiators K7927 and K8045 were involved in making such a film when they collided. It has been suggested that the film in question was entitled, "Signed with their Honour" or, "The Air War in Greece", but I have been unable to trace either, though the latter was published as a book.

My enquiries to the British Film Institute, The Film Library and The Imperial War Museum have been futile; they can find no record of this or any other film made by the RAF Film Unit at about this time. (Perhaps it was started and later abandoned.) What a pity! It would have been interesting to see if it still existed, or had disintegrated, like so much old film stock.

There is no question, however, that the accident took place; RAF crash records are available in the RAF Museum and I have spoken to Hedley Richards who was an eye-witness. Further, there is evidence to suggest that the Gladiator in the RAF Museum, Hendon, was also used during the making of the film.

* * *

Rednal, near Oswestry was the home of 61 OTU and the Gladiator must have been an anachronism in 1943, with Spitfires, Masters and Harvards amongst the many types on the unit. Indeed, in the official list of OTUs, which gives the numbers of representative types on the unit, K7927 is mentioned but is shown, in error, as a Mark 2.

Sqn Ldr Ackworth was attached to the film unit at 61 OTU. On November 24th, 1943 he authorised the use of two instructors, Flt Lt R.G. Kleinmeyer, a New Zealander, and Flt Lt K. Baghe, to fly Gladiators K7927 and K8045 for some air-to-air photography.

After the necesary filming, the pilots apparently decided to engage in a bit of formation flying. (Whether they were familiar with the Gladiator is not known.) Whilst changing formation from echelon to line-astern they collided and both pilots quickly baled out, suffering only slight injuries.

The aircraft crashed just a few hundred yards apart, near the village of Penrhos.

At the subsequent Court of Enquiry Flt Lt Kleinmeyer (pilot of K8045) was reprimanded for not keeping a proper look-out and performing unauthorised manoeuvres. Sqn Ldr Ackworth came in for his share of blame, in that he had no responsibility to authorise flights; this was the prerogative of the OC flying. The C.O. recommended the cessation of the Squadron Leader's attachment to the film unit.

* * *

Gladiator K8042, also thought to have been used during the filming, is now in the RAF Museum, Hendon.

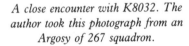

A close encounter with K8032. The author took this photograph from an Argosy of 267 squadron.

Hedley Richards was a schoolboy at the time, at nearby Llansanffraid school. During the lunch break, at about 1pm, he and his friends noticed two biplanes diving down in turn, making mock attacks on a twin-engined aircraft, possibly a Wellington or Whitley. This, naturally, held the boys spellbound for some time. Suddenly, one machine seemed to fall behind the other, two parachutes, almost simultaneously, blossoming out before the aircraft fell earthwards. The Whitley, if such it was, circled a few times and then flew off.

Hedley and his friends had seen, roughly, where the aircraft fell, so the afternoon lessons seemed interminable, the boys itching to investigate.

School over, they were off to let their parents know their plans before hurrying away. As luck would have it there were no fields to cross, back roads bringing them to Penrhos school 3 miles away.

In a wood, to the left of the road was a Gladiator, minus its engine. Impaled in the trees, not touching the ground and, with branches protruding through its fabric covered wings, it hung, guarded by soldiers. The other aircraft had fallen immediately opposite Penrhos school, in a ditch alongside the road. Hedley still remembers a strong smell of engine oil and petrol pervading the scene.

The boys then noticed activity in the field behind the school and, on going to investigate, found the engine of the first Gladiator embedded in the earth and also guarded by soldiers.

A couple of days later the lads went back but all was gone.

Hedley says that, in later life, he reflected on the narrow escape those in Penrhos school had when they were straddled by three unguided "missiles".

★ ★ ★

Penrhos school. One of the Gladiators crashed on the roadside verge on the extreme right of the picture.

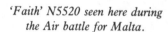

'Faith' N5520 seen here during the Air battle for Malta.

Because of its proximity to the road, the site is easily found. Of the aircraft that landed in the trees there can be no expectation of finding any remains. Undergrowth and brambles made my investigation of the aeroplane in the ditch a painstaking task and, as yet, nothing had been found.

There is still a chance, however, that evidence of this bizarre incident may come to light.

MR 1. 126/240166
MR 2. 126/239167

Note. Since preparing this book for publication the author has discovered a copy of the book *Signed with their Honour* in a Hay-on-Wye bookshop. It was first published in 1987, nearly 45 years *after* the filming!

General Dynamics F-111E 68-0070

The F-111 superceded the F-105 Super Sabre as a strike-fighter in the USAF. A far heavier aircraft, it was the first variable geometry (swing-wing) aircraft to see operational service. Powered by two TF30-P-3 turbo-fan engines of 18500 lbs thrust each, it can exceed Mach 1 (the speed of sound) from sea level to its maximum ceiling. With a practical radius of action approaching a thousand miles, which can be extended by air-to-air refuelling, it can carry over 8000 lbs of bombs.

It first flew on December 21st, 1964 and is still in service today. At one time the RAF was to be equipped with the F-111, but early teething troubles and political factors caused the order to be cancelled.

Ironically, the British aircraft built to a somewhat similar specification, the TSR-2, was also cancelled, days after its first flight.

The F-111 has flown operationally in the Far East, Libya and the Gulf with great success. In a seven month period in 1972/3, in South East Asia, F-111s flew over 4000 combat missions, sustaining only six losses.

Over 500 F-111s were manufactured during its production run.

★   ★   ★

Upper Heyford in Oxfordshire has been the home of the 20th Tactical Fighter Wing since September 12th, 1970.

On Monday, October 31st, 1977, a NATO exercise designed to test the response time of the 20th TFW began, continuing for the rest of the week. The Secretary of State for the RAF, James Wellbeloved, had informed members of the House that low flying would be taking place, by day and night, over Wales and other areas during this period. About 70 aircraft were involved, one of which was F-111E serial number 68-0070*. The crew were:

CAPT. JOHN J. SWEENEY (30) of AMSTERDAM, OHIO. Pilot.
CAPT. WILLIAM W. SMART (35) from TIERRA VERDI, FLORIDA.
Weapons Systems Officer.

Capt. Sweeney was flying behind the lead aircraft in atrocious weather conditions, with low cloud, heavy rain and strong winds. An observer in Welshpool commented, at the time, that the aircraft seemed to be flying much lower than was usual.

A local newspaper reported that Glyn Roberts of Foel Llwyd farm, was outside at the time and saw the lead aircraft fly over. A second aircraft followed, flying much lower and appeared to "Go through the trees". It was so low that Mr Roberts saw the lights quite clearly and reported that there seemed to be no fire or explosion prior to the aircraft hitting the ground.

Seconds later Mr Richard Lewis, in Pentre Bach at Foel, heard a loud roar followed by an explosion. Pieces of metal rained down on the farmhouse roof. Going outside he saw flaming fragments dropping from the sky and fires all around the field.

The aircraft had crashed a mere 250 yards from his house, making a crater about 150 feet long and 30 feet deep. He ran back to the house and dialled 999 for help. The explosion was heard 3 miles away in Llangadfan and people reported that the whole place seemed to shake with its force.

The lead aircraft was over the Great Orme at Llandudno when the crew became aware that the number 2 was missing and sent out a Mayday signal. A helicopter from RAF Valley was soon on the scene but nothing could be done for the crew who were killed instantly.

Daylight revealed a scene of utter devastation. The whole field was littered with wreckage. One engine had been blasted over two hedges and into another field by the force of the explosion. The farmhouse was intact but the roofs of nearby buildings had sustained some damage.

---

* In the USAF numbering system, the first two digits show the year in which the aircraft was ordered. In this particular instance, the aircraft was ordered in 1968 and this was the 70th aircraft contracted that year.

Pentre Bach farm, Foel, from the crash site.

Left: Fuel valve found at crash site.

A large USAF contingent soon arrived and no-one was allowed into the field. The parts of the aircraft were gathered up into the centre of the field and a USAF helicopter, using a net slung underneath, took them to a road nearby where they were taken away in trucks.

One aspect of the operation caused William Lewis, (Richard's brother) some distress. The recovery team instead of collecting the scattered remains of the crew immediately, marked them, where they were found, with little black tags. It was sometime before they were collected and Mr Lewis was worried that the farm dogs might pick them up.

The USAF team remained on the site for some weeks.

★   ★   ★

I went to Pentre Bach farm and met Mr Lewis who readily agreed to take me to the site, only a couple of hundred yards or so from the house. He was able to point out the exact spot where the aircraft finally came to rest; it is conveniently marked with a patch of bog-grass.

"You won't find anything here," said Mr Lewis. "You could have put a house into the hole. We had to get a JCB to fill it with soil from other parts of the field, so any fragments will be 30 feet down."

He left me to look over the field with my metal detector nevertheless, and dozens of fragments came to light nearby. A few interesting pieces were seen and reburied. Some had part numbers stencilled on them while others, painted red, indicated that they were part of the wing structure where the moving sections, such as flaps etc. are so coloured.

Note. Low flying at night in the F-111 is greatly assisted by the use of Terrain Following Radar and it may well have been a fault in this system which was responsible for the ensuing disaster. It should be noted, however, that during a low-level trial in Thailand, some years previously, three F-111s had been lost, probably due to fatigue failure in the tailplane actuators. This cannot be ruled out as a possible cause of this accident but it is likely that modifications would have been undertaken by this time.

MR125/981129

General Dynamics F-111Es

USAF personnel scour the field for remains of 68-0070.

Left: Mrs D. Davies and Mary Lewis hold parts of the F-111, which fell near Pentre Bach.

Republic P-47c Thunderbolt 41-6195 Coded VM-C

With, at one time, over 150 P-47s based at Atcham, the skies over mid and eastern Wales must have reverberated with the thunder of their mighty Pratt and Whitney engines. Indeed, it is surprising how few of these aircraft crashed, considering the amount of flying that took place.

Whilst flying the aircraft to the limits of its performance, the inexperience of the pilot, like that of his RAF counterparts of Hawarden and Rednal, sometimes lead to trouble. Spins in the Spitfire were not easy to control and, at low level, the Thunderbolt could prove something of a handful, often with fatal results.

★ ★ ★

On July 8th, 1944, 2nd Lt Orin Wahl found himself in just such a situation and it is pleasing to report that, on this occasion, the pilot managed to bale out and save his life. He landed safely on the hillside, injuring himself only slightly and was later found in a nearby pub downing a glass of ale.

Not that he got away scot-free, I imagine. He most likely found himself in front of his Commanding Officer trying to explain away the American Government's loss of $76,562, not including the cost of wreckage recovery. (It is lucky, I suppose, that he was not flying the P-47D, as that machine cost an extra $5000!) The aircraft crashed on moorland about 300 yards east of Aled Isaf reservoir and was, as the Recovery Officer said at the time, " . . . a complete wreck".

Lt Wahl survived the war, after completing over 100 combat missions and continued with his interrupted medical studies.

★ ★ ★

As this site is but a short walk through the heather, there are few signs of wreckage on the surface; just a bare parch scarring the hillside. Only a few years ago the ground was littered with alloy fragments but, it seems, some enthusiastic "collector" has removed the lot — a pointless exercise.

MR116/915592

During the war, civilian contractors were often used to remove wreckage from crash sites. One of those was Aber Carriers. The staff is seen here with their vehicles.

De Havilland Mosquito FB Mk VI* HJ787

At a time when most aircraft had long since forsaken wood as the main element in their construction, the Mosquito returned to this most basic material.

The fuselage, made in two halves from a sandwich of plywood with a balsa filling, was formed over moulds of concrete or wood. This had the added advantage that internal equipment could be fitted before the two sections were glued together. To keep out the elements and give a smooth finish, it was then covered with fabric, doped and then painted.

With two Rolls-Royce Merlin engines, the Mosquito could outstrip most enemy night fighters and the bomber version carried no defensive armament.

It is interesting to note that only 50 Mosquitoes were shot down by German night fighters. Using the most potent of Luftwaffe fighters, the FW190 and the jet-propelled Me262, Ob. Lt Welter of 10/NJG11 was credited with 7 of these!

Surprisingly, in 1943/4 it was also used by BOAC on the Stockholm run, carrying secret documents, mail, ball-bearings and even passengers sitting in the bomb bay.

Total production, which ended in 1950, amounted to 7781 aircraft. The Mosquito FB Mark VI fighter-bomber was armed with 4 20 mm cannon, 4 0.303 inch machine guns and could carry a 1000 lb bomb load. This, with a maximum speed of 358 mph, made it a most formidable weapon.

★ ★ ★

Mosquito FB Mk VI serial no. HJ787 was built at the main De Havilland factory at Hatfield, under contract no. 555. Delivered to the RAF on June 23rd, 1943, it survived for just one month before being categorised as 'Cat. E', i.e. scrap. It was fitted with Merlin XXIII engines and failure of the port engine, serial no. 335562, was the cause of the ensuing disaster.

No. 301 Ferry Training Unit, of 44 Group Transport Command, was based at Lyneham near Swindon. At ten past eleven on July 24th, 1943, five days after its delivery to Lyneham, HJ787 took off on a fuel consumption test. The pilot was Fg. Off. T.G. Eyre (21) who had 491 flying hours to his credit, 42 of them on Mosquitoes. His Navigator for this flight was Sgt R.A. Gordall, also 21 years old.

Two hours fifty minutes into the flight, the port engine failed and, before the pilot could feather the propeller, the engine began to hammer itself to pieces. It then caught fire, which with a wooden aircraft like the Mosquito, meant that the only course of action was for the crew to abandon the machine with some speed.

The two halves of the fuselage having equipment fitted before they are glued together at the De Havilland factory at Hatfield.

* Note: All wartime marks of aircraft and engines were expressed in Roman numerals. At the end of the war, Arabic numerals were used, thus the Mosquito Mark XXX was followed by the Mosquito Mark 34.

A Mosquito FBVI with the port engine stopped and the propeller feathered.

HJ787 crashed in the foreground; behind is Pentrenant Hall.

The aircraft was at low altitude so the pilot attempted to gain height in order to give the navigator a better chance of parachuting to safety. Sgt Gordall baled out but deployed his parachute too soon. This caught the tail of the aircraft, causing the pilot to lose control and the Mosquito crashed into a field at Pentrenant Farm, near Churchstoke, killing both crew members. The wreckage burned fiercely and soon only the metal parts remained.

*   *   *

The results of the Court of Inquiry were rather predictable. Where all crew members were killed it was very easy to blame the pilot. In this case they decided that Fg. Off. Eyre failed to carry out the correct single engine flying procedures, by not feathering the propeller quickly enough.

One cannot carry out on accident investigation 50 years after the event and when all evidence has long since gone, but it does seem unlikely that a pilot with nearly 500 hours flying experience would fail to notice an engine failure and take immediate action. The crash investigators must have found the propeller in the feathered position, so how did they know what caused the engine to break up? Perhaps the feathering mechanism was faulty, or perhaps . . . but then we are again entering the realms of conjecture. After all, if the navigator had baled out successfully both he and the pilot may well have survived.

It is unlikely that, as they pushed their tea cups aside at the Court of Inquiry, they had any idea what happened to that young crew in a burning Mosquito, in the skies above Montgomeryshire, at 2 pm on a July afternoon in 1943.

* * *

I met Mrs Ethel Webster, at her cottage near the crash site. This gritty, 75 year old lady was not at all put out by her artificial leg, the result of an accident, she told me, "whilst working in a man's world, as an HGV driver in Wiltshire".

From her kitchen window, looking through the trees that surround Pentrenant Hall, she pointed out the field where the Mosquito crashed. In her 20s at the time, she still remembers it well, telling me that all that remained of the unfortunate crew was a single flying boot. Not content with just indicating the field she insisted on coming with me up the lane to ensure that I recorded the exact spot.

Only minute fragments of the tragedy now remain and those lie under the grassy surface, where sheep now graze peacefully.

MR 137/242912

Vickers-Armstrong's Wellington Mk 1c R1286

Of the thousands of Wellingtons built, many ended their days on Operational Training Units (OTUs) and in general were considered a good aircraft for crews undergoing advanced training. The Mark 1 version with 1,000 hp Bristol Pegasus engines, however, had rather limited asymmetric performance, rectified in the Mark III which had 1,500 hp engines.

It's often forgotten, in these days of reliable jet engines, how fragile were large piston engines and complicated propeller mechanisms of the war years. Engines later benefited from the impetus given, during the war, into research for better materials.

Even in the post-war era, Hastings and Valetta aircraft spent a great deal of time stranded in foreign parts awaiting engine changes! When an engine failed on a Wellington, height could be maintained but substantial climb was usually out of the question.

The crew of Wellington R1286 found themselves in just such a situation.

* * *

The date, Friday, June 13th, 1940, was an ominous precursor of what was to come. Plt. Off. Bainbridge, with a crew of six, took off from 15 OTU Harwell, Oxfordshire, on a cross-country flight to Scotland. (Little did they know what they were to have the dubious honour of being in the 20th Wellington from that unit to crash within the last two months.)

On the return leg of the flight, the port engine began to smoke, the engine was stopped and the propeller feathered. The Captain decided to make a landing in the Isle of Man, probably at RAF Jurby.

A Wellington crew study their maps at an OTU.

Wellington R1286 crashed in the bog shown, just below the hill to the right of the picture.

Sgt Bill Breeze in flying kit.

After the crash, Bill Breeze served out the rest of the war in the Motor Transport branch. Here he is seen on a Norton motorcycle. The truck in the background is a Crossley.

The engine was checked and the oil tank refilled then, despite the misgivings of the engine mechanic, the crew, who wanted to get back to Harwell, presumably for personal reasons, decided to continue.

Shortly after resuming the homeward flight, the engine seized-up. They crossed the Welsh coast near Aberystwyth, at about 1,000 ft but a landing was increasingly imperative and, because of the paucity of airfields in Mid-Wales, decided to attempt to reach Pershore or another airfield near Worcester.

It is a moot point, easily made 50 years later from the comfort of an armchair, as to whether it would have been better to ditch near Aberystwyth or crash-land on lower ground nearby. The navigator must have been aware of the type of terrain to be covered, but they decided to go on. The die had been cast.

The pilot struggled to coax the aircraft to a higher altitude, without much success. They had flown about 10 miles inland and continued over Pontrhydfendigaid up the Teifi valley in a south-easterly direction. The ground here rises inexorably to the 1,500 foot Pen-y-Bwlch and, in avoiding nearby hills, the aircraft struck a slope with its port wing crashing into boggy ground nearby.

Both pilots were killed, on impact, when they were thrown from the aircraft and a supernumery crew member F. Sgt Powell, died on the way to Aberystwyth hospital.

The four survivors, found in the bog by men cutting peat nearby, were extricated and also taken to hospital. Sgt Bill Breeze, the rear gunner, was injured badly enough to be taken off flying duties and spent the rest of the war in a ground trade.

Fate stepped in here, as so often it does. The other three crew members, with lesser injuries, returned to flying duties and all were subsequently killed in different Wellington crashes; two of them, the navigator and the wireless operator whilst on operations in the Middle East.

Sgt Breeze, a Welshman, died only a few years ago, probably gaining nearly 50 years extra life as a result of his injuries, sustained on Friday, June 13th, 1940.

*   *   *

The metalled road ends near Pant-y-Fedwen. It is then a 2.5 mile uphill walk along the forest track to the point nearest the crash site. Once there, I do not recommend that you actually go to the site but just view the area where the tragic events described above took place. One reason for this is that it is practically impossible to pin-point an exact spot and the other is that it is in a bog.

This may seem at variance with what I said in the Introduction, about only giving exact references. However, I have spent 16 hours (not including the journey up the track) in searching three different MRs, before finally returning, in the company of two gentlemen from Aberystwyth. John Davies and Ivor Richards, who went there a few years ago, brought back a piece of what appears to be a trim tab and which is now in the keeping of Aberystwyth ATC. They took me to the area, but demurred to venturing too far into the bog. Ivor, who had a red and white surveyors rod with him, demonstrated why.

Pushing the rod into the mossy ground, with hardly any pressure at all, he showed just how easily it slipped down the five feet or so of its length.

If you think that a five mile walk is not worth the effort required just to view the site (a mountain bike would prove invaluable) go to Strata Florida just the same, it is only a couple of miles short of Pant-y-Fedwen and well worth a visit.

This Abbey, built in 1164 was the Welsh contribution to the Cistertian order and a fine Norman-style arch and tiled pavements remain.

Wales' best loved poet Dafydd ap Gwilym, who died in 1370, lies buried here under a yew tree.

MR 147/782628

Flight of Eagles
North American P-51D Mustang 44-72340

The Mustang could be reasonably described as the Saviour of the US 8th Air Force Bomber Command.

By the autumn of 1943 any ideas that large formations of B-17s and B-24s could defend themselves on bombing missions over Germany had been largely dispelled. The attack on the ball-bearing works at Schweinfurt, (a round trip of about 1200 miles) on September 27th, 1943 resulted the loss of 60 aircraft, with the P47 Thunderbolt escort not having sufficient range to go further than Aachen, less than half-way.

On December 5th, 1943 the first escort mission was flown by Mustangs and later, with large external fuel tanks (made in Britain) they were able to stay with the bombers all the way to the target. Eventually, on March 4th, 1944 they reached Berlin itself.

It was the salvation of the bombers and the beginning of the end of the Luftwaffe fighter force.

★　★　★

The Mustang story had started four years earlier, in early 1940, when the British Purchasing Commission were very impressed by the performance of the Curtiss P40. They asked the North American Company, who had never produced a fighter aircraft of their own design, to manufacture the P40 for the RAF, unless they could produce a better design of their own in the time it would have taken to tool-up for P40 production.

After much frantic activity at the factory, the prototype with chief test pilot Vance Breeze at the controls, took-off for the first time on October 26th, 1940 from Mines Field, California.

Although the RAF took delivery of some 2,600 Mustangs, the majority, about, 12,000 aircraft, went to the USAAF. The P-51D version of the Mustang was powered by a Rolls-Royce Merlin engine of 1,695 hp built by Packard in the USA. It had a maximum speed of 437 mph, a range with external tanks of over 2000 miles and was armed with six 0.5 inch Browning machine guns.

★　★　★

Before the USA entered the war, a number of American citizens keen to fly high performance aircraft, decided to come over to Britain and join the RAF.

They fought bravely in the Battle of Britain, three of them losing their lives in the process.

Eventually, they formed three squadrons, Nos 71, 121 and 133, the 'Eagle' squadrons; although all the ground crew were British). Equipped with Spitfire Mk. Vbs they flew on operations with the RAF until, on September 29th, 1942 they were handed over, complete with their Spitfires to the USAAF. They became 334, 335 and 336 Fighter Squadrons of the 4th Fighter Group.

Not long after this, they were re-equipped with the Republic P47 Thunderbolt. This aircraft weighed over twice as much as the Spitfire, proving so much of a handful, that mock combats between the two types were banned after a number of fatal P47 crashes.

Later they were again re-equipped, but this time with P-51 Mustangs, one of the finest piston-engined fighters ever produced.

★　★　★

P-51D Mustang 44-72340 was part of the 335th Fighter squadron (ex. 121 squadron RAF) and was based at Debden in Essex, a former Battle of Britain airfield.

On May 17th, 1945, just 8 days after the end of the war in Europe, aircraft of the squadron were flying in formation at 25000 feet over Wales, possibly en route to one of the USAAF's maintenance bases in Lancashire.

Suddenly, the aircraft piloted by Captain Richard L. Tannehill of Stockton, California, fell out of the

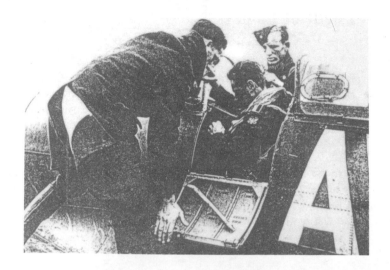

Left: The American pilot of an RAF 'Eagle' squadron is strapped into his Spitfire by RAF groundcrew.

A P-51D Mustang.

Aran Fawddwy from the Bala-Dolgellau road. 44-72340 crashed in the distant forest.

formation, the pilot probably unconscious because of lack of oxygen. With the throttle open, the aircraft was soon diving at high speed, probably at over 400 mph. There are slightly conflicting accounts, none of which from actual eye-witnesses, as to what happened next. One view is that the aircraft crashed onto the Bala-Dolgellau road with wreckage scattered on both sides. A more believable version, in view of the present disposition of the wreckage, is that it crashed about 2 miles east of the road.

P-51s being towed by RAF Fordson lorries through the Mersey Tunnel from Liverpool docks.

Wreckage of 44-42340 on the hillside.

One thing is certain! As the speed of the aircraft exceeded its design limitations it began to disintegrate, the engine falling a considerable distance away from the rest of the wreckage. Indeed, it remained officially undiscovered in the Afan-Ty-Cerrig until 1975, 30 years later, when an RAF Mountain Rescue Team found it.

* * *

The area was planted with conifers by the Forestry Commission over 40 years ago, making any search for remains particularly difficult. However, part of the forest to the south of the river has been felled revealing scattered wreckage. Unfortunately, P-51 components do not seem to have the proliferation of part numbers and inspection stamps found on British aircraft and most marked parts have been removed. It is an unfortunate fact of life that aircraft of the USAAF seem to attract more attention than that of our own RAF (which operated under the cover of darkness in more than one sense) and crash remains are no exception.

The river itself is a fruitful area to search, containing, as it does, quite large fragments.

Of course, it is unlikely that all the wreckage fell on just the south side of the river and there must be much remaining in the forest, but a look over the fence into the gloomy, almost impenetrable interior, is enough to put off any but the most intrepid searcher.

The Afan-Ty-Cerrig itself is wonderful; on a hot summers day it could almost be the tropical rain forest. The slopes leading down to the river are a riot of wild flowers and the banks are covered with deep, warm, mosses. A F.C. track leads up through the forest and ends within a few hundred yards of the crash site, but it is a two mile uphill walk to get there.

MR 125/846234

Handley-Page Hampden Mk 1 P1294

The Hampden was the last twin-engined bomber to enter service during the expansion programme prior to the war, the others being the Wellington, Whitley and Blenheim. It had the speed of a light bomber but carried a much heavier bomb load.

The forward fuselage was deep and narrow, the pilot's cockpit being similar to that of a fighter. The tail, carried on a thin tapering boom, gave it the nickname 'Flying Suitcase' or 'Flying Panhandle'. It was powered by two Bristol Pegasus engines of 1000 hp each. These engines are mentioned elsewhere in this book, in relation to the Wellington but, whereas in the 'Wimpy' they were required to propel a 28,000 lb aeroplane, in the Hampden the loaded weight was some 10,000 lbs less. Some of the weight saving was due to the fact that no power-operated gun turrets were fitted.

Attacks from the rear, from both above and below, could be countered by twin 0.303 inch machine guns, in dorsal and ventral positions. This type of attack was expected and indeed practiced, by our own fighters before the war, a flight of three aircraft lining up behind an "enemy" bomber, each in turn taking pot-shots at it.

During attacks by Hampdens on German positions the Luftwaffe, unfortunately, used different tactics. (Especially in the Norwegian campaign.) The Bf110 twin-engined fighter, a failure in the Battle of Britain, could just fly alongside Hampdens, the rear gunner spraying the cockpit and engines in complete safety. The Hampdens rear armament could not traverse sufficiently to afford any defence.

The Hampden, like other British bombers, was soon assigned to the night bomber role, where it performed well until its withdrawal from this task in 1942. (Thereafter it continued to serve in other capacities.)

The Hampden first flew on June 21st, 1936. By December 1943, the last squadron, then serving in Coastal Command in an anti-shipping role, were replaced by Beaufighters. 1270 Hampdens were built in Britain by Handley-Page and English Electric of Preston and a further 160 in Canada.

* * *

In October of 1941, No. 14 OTU, of 6 Group Bomber Command, was based at Cottesmore. On the 30th of that month Plt. Off. G.D. Kerr, with Sergeants I.M. Williams, D. Tatton and H. Playforth was detailed to fly a daylight cross-country training flight in Hampden P1294. He had already flown 41 hours on this type and a further 85 on other aircraft during earlier training.

They took off from Cottesmore and during the flight encountered cloudy conditions. This, in itself, should have presented no problems for a pilot with 24 hours instrument flying in his log book. In turbulent conditions however, the pilot was thrown forward in his seat onto the control column, causing the aircraft to "bunt"*.

A Handley-Page Hampden of 44 sqn RAF.

38

* A downward loop.

P1294 crashed in the foreground, bringing down the power cables crossing the field.

Pilot Officer Kerr struggled to regain control but the aircraft continued to gain speed relentlessly. By the time it emerged from the cloud, design limitations being exceeded, both wings sheered off and it crashed. In a field near Llynclas farm, just a hundred yards or so from the Oswestry-Bala road, at 12.30 pm it burnt out, killing all four crew members.

The later Court of Inquiry concluded that there was evidence of the pilot not being strapped in properly but this does not seem to have been wholly his fault.

Safety belts should, apparently have been a personal issue to all pilots, as stated in the relevant Air Publication, but this was not adhered to. During the Inquiry the recommendation that the Publication be amended was rejected, on the grounds that AP3024, covering the subject of Flight Safety, was shortly to be issued.

The later Defect Report, No. 110 D4/11, stated that the "wings failed in download, due to overstressing in a high speed dive, after loss of control".*

★   ★   ★

Memory is a funny thing. I was lucky enough in this case to meet someone who, as a schoolboy, saw the Hampden crash. He told me that it came over the hill, from the north, with its engines roaring and looked as though the pilot was trying to make a crash-landing. He was prevented from doing so, my informant said, by electric power lines, which the aircraft hit, causing it to crash into the field and burst into flames. Passers by on the road could clearly see the crew struggling to free themselves but were unable to get near enough to help because of the intense heat.

Study of the Accident Records, however, does not bear out this eyewitness report. If the wings had sheared off there is absolutely no way in which the aircraft could be controlled, much less crash landed. The records must surely be correct, as the wings would have been found away from the main wreckage. The electric lines, though brought down in the crash, would have had no bearing on the outcome. There were a few houses near the site and, doubtless, someone saw the aircraft burning, whether anyone was close enough to see the crew is unlikely.

From the evidence it would appear to me that an aircraft crashing into the ground at high speed, probably in an inverted position would result in the instant death of all on board.

I have no reason to doubt that my informant saw the aircraft crash. The engines would certainly have been roaring as the wingless machine plunged earthwards. Local hearsay in the months and years after the event, have, seemingly, caused distortions to creep in. Now, 55 years later, it is hard to separate fact from fiction. (There are many events which took place in my life 50 years ago but, for the life of me, I could not describe them in detail.)

★   ★   ★

* On the 8th of the same month, Hampden P1271 crashed in similar circumstances killing all the crew.

The field where P1294 crashed is owned by the Lloyd family of Llynclas farm. After gaining their permission, I searched the area where the electricity cables cross the field. Despite it having been ploughed innumerable times since the war, dozens of minute fragments of metal and perspex can still be found. I was lucky enough to pick up one small piece which had the prefix '52' used by Handley-Page for the Hampden, stamped on it. I also found an Army greatcoat brass button, badly corroded. (Torn from the coat of a soldier guarding the crash site at the time? Who knows.)

MR 126/278241

Avro Lincoln B Mk 2 RF511

The Lincoln was the successor to the Lancaster in Bomber Command, although it arrived too late to see active service during WW11. Initially it was to be known as the Lancaster IV but, as its design became different in most areas from the Lancaster, a new name was adopted. What more appropriate than Lincoln, near to most Bomber Command airfields and whose cathedral was a landmark for so many returning crews.

Powered by 4 Rolls-Royce 'Merlin' engines of 1,680 hp the Lincoln had a maximum speed of 295 mph and an all-up weight some 7,000 lbs greater than the Lancaster. The defensive armament was upgraded by the substitution of the rifle calibre 0.303″ Brownings of the Lancaster with 0.5″ machine guns, a long overdue change. Some models had a Bristol mid-upper turret housing 20mm cannon, though this turret was later removed.

An interesting point here is that, after the war, it was found that German night-fighters had been making their attacks undetected and, in some cases, with upward firing cannon, from underneath Lancasters. This enabled them to take their time in aiming for the fuel tanks in the wings, causing the bombers to explode in spectacular, horrific fashion. So litle knowledge did Bomber Command have of this, that it was thought the Germans possessed some kind of anti-aircraft device designed to sap the morale of bomber crews. This imagined weapon was even given the name "Scarecrow" and only after the war had ended was the bitter truth revealed that these "Scarecrows" were indeed exploding bombers.

An Avro Lincoln B2.

Lincoln B2 showing the mid-upper turret with two 20mm cannon and the rear turret with two 0.5 inch guns. The bulge below the turret covers the Automatic gun-laying radar.

It is surprising that the Lincoln, although it could have a single ventral gun, had no proper turret fitted underneath, even if it meant re-locating the H2S* radar.

Total production of the Lincoln in the UK was 528 aircraft. The only operational action it saw was in Malaya, against the Communist terrorists and in Kenya during the Mau-Mau uprising. Here there was no fighter opposition, so the lack of an under turret was never a liability.

The Lincoln finally left RAF service in 1963. About half the aircraft were manufactured by Armstrong-Whitworth (makers of the "Whitley") and RF511 was one of those.

* * *

After the war OTUs were renamed OCUs (Operational Conversion Units). Here crews trained on other aircraft learned to operate different types.

No. 230 OCU, of 1 Group Bomber Command, was based at Scampton near Lincoln. This, it will be remembered, was the war-time home of 617 squadron, The "Dambusters". (The grave of Guy Gibson's dog, Nigger, killed on the day prior to the dams raid, is in front of one of the hangars to this day.)

In the 1950s the RAF experimented with a new rank system for NCO aircrew. The old ranks of Warrant Officer, Flight Sergeant and Sergeant, became Master Pilot/Navigator/Gunner etc. equivalent to Warrant Officer and other ranks became Pilot/Nav/Gunner 2 and 3. This clumsy system did not last long, except for the Master (W/O) rank which still exists.

* * *

On March 15th, 1950, the crew of Lincoln RF511 was briefed for a night navigational exercise.
The crew consisted:

> Sqn Ldr T.L. SHORE, Pilot
> Flt Lt C.A. LINDSAY, Navigator
> Eng. 2 R.A. FORESBY
> Sig. 3 H.M. CHARMAN
> Gunner 2 G.L. CUNLEY
> Gunner 2 R.F. WOOD

On completion of the exercise the Captain was informed that the weather at Scampton was below limits and the aircraft was diverted to RAF Valley in Anglesey.

The Air Traffic Control Officer at Valley told the Captain to steer a course of 010 degrees as part of the let-down procedure. This would have taken the aircraft out over the sea in a northerly direction. The pilot, however, took up a heading of 110 degrees, taking the aircraft directly toward the Carneddau.

He began his descent through 5 to 7 eighths cloud, during the course of which he informed the ATCO at Valley no less than five times that he was steering 010°.

It has to be said at this point that Sqn Ldr Shore was, reputedly, a rather headstrong person and other crew members may have been wary of pointing out his error. It is surprising that the navigator did not correct him, as he had his own compass but he may well have been operating the "Rebecca"* set at the time.

At 0225 hours the aircraft flew into the mountainside at about 2500 feet. It exploded and burned fiercely, killing all the crew members.

* * *

At the subsequent Inquiry it was decided that the pilot had misread the compass and that, in future, Flight Engineeers would be trained to monitor compass readings.

The waters of the Court of Inquiry were muddied slightly by the fact that the ATCO at Valley was Polish and the C in C stated that it was not advisable to have a non-pure English speaker at Master Diversion Airfields.

* H2S was an airborne radar for identifying ground features.

This was not, however, considered to be a contributory factor, but the fact that the pilot did not have a current instrument rating *may* have been relevant.

The aircraft had been airborne for 6 hours 15 minutes at the time of the accident.

*   *   *

Unless you are a fit hill walker, allow yourself plenty of time, say 6 hrs (or, if you include Wellington DV800 on the same trip, 7 hrs) for this walk. Don't let this put you off, as this is a spectacular area.

Start at the Welsh Water pumping station at MR 115/638659, the main feature to follow being the river (Afon Llanfar). Because of rain and terrain in general, this is not always possible and you will have to deviate to avoid boggy ground, especially in wet weather. The main topographical feature, however, is Mynydd Du to your right. This is a sheer black cliff, rising to nearly 2000 feet and appearing even higher because of a deep hollow at its base. The area is sometimes called 'Black Ladders', presumably because of the vertical lines in the rock face. This mountain, though lower than the Carneddau Dafydd and Llewelyn in front of you, will dominate your whole day and if you come away unimpressed I would be very surprised.

After a couple of hours the stream will branch off to the left; this is the Nant Ddu, which may not be noticed in wet, or, paradoxically, in very dry weather. Continue on until the going gets steeper and the next branch of the stream, the Nant Fach, will lead right up to the site. Although very steep it requires no rock climbing, just good old sweat!

The wreckage is strewn dramatically all the way from the site, at about 2500 feet, right down to the stream. Masses of debris, including superchargers, undercarriage legs, parts of the main spar, molten alloy and thousands of other pieces testifying to the terrible impact of a 35 ton, four engined bomber, flying at 200 mph, hitting a massive immovable rock face.

MR 115/679639

The view of Ysgolion Duon from the crash site.

A supercharger from RF511 lies in a mountain stream below the impact point.

Republic P-47D Thunderbolt 42-7960: A Short History

By 1944 the USAAF base at Atcham, near Shrewsbury, was fully engaged in practising low-level flying prior to the pilots being posted to operational squadrons.

At one time, in 1944, there were 150 P-47s at Atcham, home of the 495th Fighter Training Group, or Air Force Station No. 342 as it was officially known.

The P-47 Thunderbolt was a particularly potent weapon in the ground attack role. A large, single-seat fighter, powered by a Pratt and Whitney Double Wasp radial engine of 2300 hp, it could attain a speed of 427 mph, and could carry rockets or bombs in addition to its fixed armament of eight 0.5 inch machine guns.

★   ★   ★

Records show that P-47D 42-7960 left the factory of Farmingdale, New York, on March 19th, 1943, costing the US Government the princely sum of $76,562.

In New York harbour, on April 7th, 1943, it was loaded as deck cargo on a ship bound for Liverpool. On arrival, it was transported, through the streets of the city, to a nearby base where it was assembled and fitted with operational equipment.

It was then allocated to the 61st Fighter Squadron of the 56th Fighter Group based at Halesworth, Suffolk.

There, it became the personal "mount" of Capt. James R. Carter, Blue Flight leader and an "Ace" in his own right, having six confirmed air victories. The aircraft was coded HV-J at this time. Capt. Carter was later promoted to Major and became the Squadron C.O.

(Col. Gabreski, a top scoring ace of the USAAF, belonged to the 61st F.S.)

★   ★   ★

42-7960, having had its share of combat, was then relegated to the training role. (Combat placed extreme stresses on the airframe and aircraft often had the initials "WW", denoting 'War Weary', on their records.)

On the morning of July 28th, 1944, 2nd Lt Arthur C. Jenkins of the 552 Fighter Training Squadron, 495 FTG, took off from Atcham on an instrument and aerobatic fight. His number 2 was Lt Reese, in another P-47.

Weather around the base at the time was generally good but the pair soon ventured westwards, where the Welsh hills were covered with low, scudding cloud.

On entering cloud Lt Jenkins decided to climb through it but became disorientated and lost altitude in the process. He emerged from the cloud at very low level and, seeing a house ahead, made a steep turn in order to avoid it. In doing so the aircraft hit the ground just a few hundred yards from the house, ploughing through a hedge into a potato field. The engine broke away and the aircraft disintegrated as it skidded along the ground. Lt Jenkins was killed instantly.

Meanwhile, up above, Lt Reese, realising the danger, turned onto a reciprocal heading and returned safely to Atcham.

★   ★   ★

The house, so narrowly avoided by Lt Jenkins, was Pencroellyn, near Llanfair Caereinion. The farmer, John Richard and Catherine his wife, lived there with their stepson David Watkins. Mr Watkins was tending the horses in the stable at the time. He heard aircraft overhead but took little notice, until there was a loud bang nearby. Looking out of the stable he saw the smoke and flames and, unlikely as it seems now, thought that it was an incendiary bomb dropped by an enemy aircraft! His mother, however, realised what had actually happened and rushed out with buckets of water in an attempt to extinguish the flames. When they managed to locate the pilot his headless body was still strapped in the seat.

A P47 Thunderbolt.

42-79260 Taxies out.

A group of USAAF P47 pilots 'Ace' Col. F. Gabreski is on the extreme left.

The indentation near the hedge marks the impact point of 42-7960.

Lt Jenkins is buried in the US cemetery near Cambridge.

As news spread around the countryside, the farm was inundated with sightseers, taking away pieces of the wreckage as souvenirs. "There were more people than at Welshpool Show," said David Watkins.

The main wreckage was moved by tractor to the road and loaded onto lorries. The US Army salvage team stayed on the site for two weeks and there was much bartering between the family and the Americans. The Richards not having seen tinned fruit for some considerable time took this in exchange for chickens. (One G.I. actually cooked his on the spot, in his steel helmet!)

Compensation was paid by the Ministry of Agriculture for damage to crops and for a calf that had to be put down because of a broken leg. It amounted to about £35!

Next day, Lt Reese, pilot of the other aircraft, visited the site and came up to see the Observers in post P3 who had plotted the movements of the aircraft.

★   ★   ★

Pencroellyn now lies empty, the land around it being owned by a nearby farm. Permission was given to look around the field and quite a few pieces of small wreckage, some marked with the "89" prefix used on the P47, were found.

From this site, looking over to the north, Moel Bentyrch can be seen. This is where Thunderbolt 42-75090 met its fate on January 1st, 1944.

MR 125/052054

General Aircraft Hamilcar HH922

In these days of high-tech military aircraft, the glider may seem a most unlikely craft in which to go to war. It is seen as a graceful, delicate, one or two seater aircraft, suitable for sporting and leisure use, yet during WW2 it was used in large numbers as a military transport.

The use of the glider has many advantages: Parachuted troops tend to drift and become scattered, whereas gliders can be concentrated in a small area and carry more equipment.

Gliders can be very basic aircraft which, except for training, are used only once. Furthermore, they can be released some distance from the target and make a silent approach.

It has been recorded that a light military glider, released at about 10000 feet, can glide for about 30 miles, depending on wind speed and direction. In practice, they were usually released at a much lower altitude. The towing aircraft can also carry cargo which can be dropped by parachute.

The glider gained much favour in Germany between the wars when there were strict limits on the number and types of powered aircraft which could be built.

It was the Germans who made first use of them during WW2, culminating in their capture of Crete when 700 transport aircraft, mainly Junkers 52/3Ms and 80 gliders, flew in 15000 troops to overcome the island's defences. This also showed up their limitations, mainly that complete mastery of the air is essential if losses are to be kept at acceptable levels. As it was, about 130 transport aircraft and gliders were shot down, in Crete, by anti-aircraft fire and the few RAF fighters available at the time.

For the crossing of the Rhine, on March 24th, 1945, the Allies employed 4,616 powered aircraft and 1320 gliders.

The RAF still paid lip-service to the glider technique after the war, when its new twin engined transport, the Valetta, was fitted with facilities for towing. Shortly afterwards, however, the glider disappeared from service.

* * *

The Airspeed Horsa and the American built Waco CG-4A Hadrian were the two main types of glider used on Allied airborne operations. Neither of these aircraft could carry heavy loads but this deficiency was remedied with the arrival of the Hamilcar.

Built by General Aircraft Ltd of Hanworth, Middlesex, it had a wingspan of 110 feet and could carry a seven ton tank. (The only Allied glider able to do so.) Of the 412 Hamilcars constructed, only 22 were produced by GA. The remainder were built by sub-contractors, mainly the Birmingham Railway Carriage and Wagon Company.

The Germans too experimented with giant gliders but, hampered by the lack of 4 engined towing aircraft, resorted to using 3 twin engined fighters. This was a most delicate, if not hazardous procedure and 2 Heinkel III twin engined bombers, joined together to form one aircraft, were later used. Eventually they fitted six engines to the gliders as the only way to make them a practical proposition. Even so, the Me323 Gigant, as it was known, was never a complete success.

The Hamilcar was crewed by two members of the Army Glider Pilot Regiment, or ex RAF pilots seconded to the Army for that duty. It was towed by either the Short Stirling or the Handley-Page Halifax, four-engined bombers modified for airborne forces operations.

* * *

Tarrant Rushton, Dorset, was one of the airfields of No. 38 Group RAF from which the D Day airborne assault was launched in 1944 and training was in progress for the Rhine crossing in March 1945.

At 0945 on February 11th, 1945 a Halifax, towing Hamilcar HH922 took-off on a training flight. The glider's crew were:

First pilot: Staff Sgt R. Tillings
Second pilot: Staff Sgt M. Wright.

Just over 2 hours later, the combination ran into cloud and mist and Sgt Tillings was unable to see the

The General Aircraft Hamilcar.

The Me321, German equivalent of the Hamilcar, being towed by two HeIII bombers joined together to form one aircraft with five engines.

Mark III and Mark VII Halifaxes prepare to tow 48 Hamilcars on Operation Varsity, The Rhine crossing, March 1945.

towing aircraft. In a case like this, if the glider pilot is not to endanger both aircraft by his actions, he only has recourse to the Cable Angle Indicator. By knowing the angle of the towing cable he is able to judge his position relative to the towing aircraft. Sgt Tillings released his harness and leaned forward to see the cable indicator but here the accident report is hazy as to whether (a) he could see it, or (b) whether one was fitted anyway! However, he was being towed through cloud at over 100 mph not knowing where he was going. The intercom between the two aircraft had become unserviceable, so he took the decision to cast off the towing cable.

Emerging through the haze, he was confronted, by steeply rising fields leading to a hilltop. It soon became obvious that he would not be able to reach the top and would have to make an uphill landing. Coming over a farmhouse roof, the aircraft struck the rising ground, shearing off its undercarriage. A wing struck an ash tree and the glider slewed around, crashing into the next field.

Both crew members were slightly injured and taken to hospital. An Army guard arrived and made their

Alfred Brown, of Cwmarron farm,
with a stainless steel fragment
which hung on the wall of his
father's farmhouse.
The Hamilcar ladder is still in use.

Fragments of the Hamilcar
structure lay in the bracken, adjacent
to the field where the glider crashed.

base in the barn of Castle Cwmarron farm. The RAF salvage team came later but there was little of importance to remove. The effort required to take away what would most likely become firewood, was not really worth the trouble and so the wreckage remained on the hillside.

Over the following months most of the wreckage disappeared, to be used to block gaps in hedges and hold up wilting barns. What remained gently rotted away in the bracken filled ditches until, fifty years later, only metal parts remain in the field.

At the subsequent Court of Inquiry the pilot of the towing aircraft was adjudged to be to blame for towing the glider into deteriorating weather, rather than altering course. It was also stated that the glider pilot should have had his harness secured at the time of landing, which would have reduced his injuries.

★ ★ ★

I visited Castell Cwmarron farm and met Mr Alfred Brown whose father lived there at the time of the crash. He took me up to the site, showing me the stump of the ash tree struck by the Hamilcar in its attempt to land in the next field. Lying in a ditch were a number of massive stainless steel plates with steel bolts going through them. These originally clamped together the large timbers used in the construction of the wings. They bore the inspection stamps of the Birmingham Railway Carriage Co; the timbers have long since rotted away.

On return to the farm, Mr Brown showed me a gleaming stainless steel plate, about a yard long, which had been hanging in the house, while the wooden ladder, used in the Hamilcar to reach the flight deck, has been doing sterling service in the barn for the last fifty years. His father buried some of the larger pieces of the aircraft many years ago.

Sepecat Jaguar GR1 XZ386

SEPECAT, a joint venture between the British Aircraft Corporation and Dassault/Breguet of France, was formed to produce the Jaguar strike-fighter. Four hundred were to be built, divided equally between the RAF and the French Air Force. Thirty five of those for the RAF were for the two-seat training version, whilst the majority were the GR1 single-seat model.

The first British built aircraft, XW560, made its maiden flight from Warton in Lancashire on October 29th, 1969. (The same airfield from which the renowned Canberra made its first flight some 20 years earlier). Delays, however, meant that the first RAF squadron to be equipped with Jaguars did not become operational until August 1974.

Powered by two Rolls-Royce/Turbomeca Adour turbo-fan engines of 7,140 lbs thrust each, the Jaguar has a speed, at 32000 feet, of 1057 mph. At its more usual operating height of 1000 feet, this is reduced to 820 mph. It is armed with two Aden 30mm cannon and can carry a bomb load of up to 10000 lbs.

The Jaguar's remarkable low-level capabilities and excellent manoeuvrability proved a great asset in the Gulf war and, at the time of writing, flies regular patrols over northern Iraq and Bosnia.

Production of the Jaguar was completed in 1977. June 1987 was a particularly bad month for the RAF with 2 Tornados and 2 Jaguars crashing within a 3 week period, XZ386 was one of those.

* * *

As mentioned in the foreword, this book is mainly concerned with wartime air crashes. As in the previous volume, I include a couple of modern day jet crashes to show that malfunction and pilot error can still take their toll. I have not, however, included any that occurred in the last 15 years or so, because I feel that it would be insensitive and might cause distress to relatives.

I include the crash of XZ386, at the time of writing only eight years earlier, because I feel that the pilot, Flt Lt Ian Hill (41) displayed courage in the finest traditions of the RAF. He saved the lives of those on the ground in the path of his stricken aircraft and, in doing so, lost his own life.

* * *

On the morning of June 24th, 1987, Flt Lt Hill of 226 OCU, in the company of two other Jaguars, took off from RAF Chivenor, Devon, for an ultra low-level exercise. At the tiny village of Aberedw, just before 11 am, Mrs Dilys Davies and the sub-postmaster Ted Gartery saw the aircraft come over the tops of the houses. They watched, transfixed, as, with pieces of the Jaguar flying off, the pilot obviously attempted to avoid the village.

Farmer John Davies, of Pantau farm, was busily spraying nettles. He ran for his life when a 'fireball' flew over his head, as the aircraft exploded in the next field. Parts of the Jaguar were hurled more than 150 yards, landing only a short distance from the terrified farmer. ("He never really got over that moment," his widow told me, in 1995.)

The villagers so moved by the sacrifice of the pilot, set up a fund for a permanent memorial to be placed in Aberedw church. Later, the pilot's widow made arrangements with the farmer for a simple stone memorial to be built amongst the rocks at Pantau farm, where her husband died.

* * *

Pantau farm now lies deserted. Since John Davies' death, his wife, Freda, lives with her son, in nearby Ryscog farm. Terry readily agreed to take me to the site, showing me the exact place where the aircraft crashed, just a short distance from the farm house. Taking me to the memorial stone nearby, he left me to look around.

Small fragments abound but this is no place to collect souvenirs, but rather to dwell upon the courage of Ian Hill, who gave his life for others.

As I returned to my car, deep in thought, there came the sound of an aircraft flying from the east at low-level and, as if in salute, a Jaguar GR1 roared overhead.

Jaguar GR1

*Flt Lt Ian D. Hill shortly
before his death.*

*PHOTOGRAPHS TAKEN ON
DAY OF THE CRASH.
The tail and one engine lay
in the meadow.*

One engine blasted into a nearby tree.

(Extract from Obituary in RAF Lossiemouth magazine)

Flight Lieutenant Ian Hill (1946-1987)

Flt Lt Ian 'Idi' Hill died tragically in a flying accident near Builth Wells on June 24th. No. 226 OCU and RAF Lossiemouth have lost an outstanding friend, and the Service has lost one of its most respected and experienced pilots.

He was posted to 226 OCU in 1981 as an instructor on the Jaguar, notching up nearly 2500 hours on the type and providing an invaluable source of specialist knowledge on the aircraft and its peculiarities. There is not a pilot flying the Jaguar in the RAF today who has not been grateful for Ian's patient instruction and advice.

Outside the Jaguar force, Ian will best be remembered for his brilliant display flying during the 1986 season. His singleton Jaguar display earned the admiration of the onlookers and the respect of other Jaguar pilots.

★   ★   ★

The following is an extract from a letter written to the author by Ian Hill's widow, and printed with her permission.

"The photograph is a copy of one I keep on display at my home - to me it is the serious professional side of Ian, and the reason he lived and died. He absolutely loved flying.

I had the memorial erected on the spot where Ian died because that was his wish. On one or two occasions when friends had been killed and he had a beer or two too many he said "put a cairn on the hillside where I kill myself". Mr Davies, the farmer, and his family were extremely kind to me and built the cairn on the hillside for me.

"Indeed, I will never forget the great kindness and sharing of my grief that I experienced from all the people of Aberedw — it helped me cope with the trauma of it all."

★   ★   ★

Flt Lt Ian Hill is buried at Lossiemouth. On his grave stone are the first two lines of "High Flight" by J.G. Magee Jr.

    'Oh, I have slipped the surly bonds of earth
     And danced the skies on laughter-silvered wings.'

MR 147/084467   **Memorial MR 147/084468**

Memorial where Ian Hill died.
Sheep graze on the crash site.

The tree where the engine landed is on the right of the picture.

Pantau church. A memorial has been placed by villagers in a nearby wall.

Dornier 17Z3 Werke No. 2682 coded 7T + LL

The Do17 was built to meet a requirement of the German airline, Deutsche Luft Hansa, for a high speed mail and passenger aircraft, making its first flight in 1934.

The slim fuselage earned the nickname, 'The Flying Pencil' later in its career. This characteristic caused its rejection by DLH, as the six passengers could only reach their seats with some difficulty.

The German Air Ministry, having evaluated the machine as a possible medium bomber, started production in 1936, the first squadrons in KG153 and KG155 receiving their aircraft in mid-1937.

Like the British Blenheim, the Do17 made an impressive public debut, outstripping French fighter aircraft, (probably Dewoitine D510 monoplanes) by a considerable margin.

The Do17F first saw active service with the Condor Legion during the Spanish civil war in 1938, but by the outbreak of World War 2 it had largely been replaced by the improved 'Z' version.

The Do17Z, powered by two Bramo 'Fafnir' radial engines of 1000 hp each, had a speed of 224 mph, a range of 721 miles with a 1,102 lb bomb load and a defensive armament of six 7.9 mm machine guns. Various sub-series were used during the Battle of Britain, the aircraft later becoming known as the Dornier 215, (similar in most respects).

The Do17Z3 was the reconnaissance version which carried cameras in addition to its bomb load.

* * *

The official period of the Battle of Britain was from July 11th to October 30th, 1940, but, by October, most heavy attacks on British cities took place at night.

Photographic flights had, of course, to be carried out in daylight, an extremely hazardous operation. The only other Luftwaffe aircraft appearing in these pages was shot down whilst on a similar daylight mission.

7T + LL* belonged either to KG606 3rd Staffel, or to Kusterfleiger Gruppe. (The records are rather hazy on this point but in either case it was certainly a naval reconnaissance unit.)

* * *

October 16th, 1940 was a quiet day, with widespread fog over France and Germany, so few German aircraft violated British airspace. Seven of those were shot down, one of which was 7T + LL.

The crew of this aircraft, briefed to bomb and photograph targets in the Merseyside area were:

LEUTNANT ZUR SEE* HEINZ HAVEMANN, Pilot   * Literally "Of the Sea", i.e. Naval.
UNTEROFFIZER KARL HOLSCHER
UNTEROFFIZER GERHARD LOCKNITZ
GEFREITER RUDI FAERMAN

They took off from their base at Brest in Western France in late afternoon and, on nearing the target, the aircraft was hit by ground fire.

Having failed to reach the target and with a damaged aircraft, the pilot might well have jettisoned the bomb load in order to lighten the aircraft and make good his escape. He decided, however, to fly at low level, up the Vale of Clwyd, deviating to the west of Denbigh. Whilst flying through the mist, the aircraft crashed into a field a few hundred yards from the farmhouse of Hafod Wen.

There was an explosion which wrecked the aircraft, killing all crew members. This did not, amazingly, set off the bomb load which remained, undisturbed even during the removal of the surface wreckage, for some 43 years. Then, in 1983, a recovery group gained permission to excavate the site, coming to an abrupt halt when they discovered the unexploded bombs!

A Royal Engineers bomb disposal team, lead by Lt Alan Miller, arrived from their base at Chatham to deal with the situation.

* The aircraft markings on Luftwaffe aircraft are in two groups: That in front of the national black cross show the Gruppe, or Geschwader, (a large formation, consisting of a number of Staffels). That painted behind the cross indicate the Staffel, or squadron, together with the aircraft's individual letter. Luftwaffe markings, however, are a rather complicated study in themselves.

A formation of Do17Zs.

A German pilot points to his improvised unit badge.

Luftwaffe aircrew prepare, whilst in the background a Do17Z has an engine run-up.

Below: 7T + LL crashed in the field beside the old farm building.

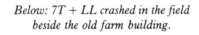

They found some ten 50 kg bombs (a full bomb load for the Do17Z), which they injected with fluid to stabilise the explosive. Then, taking the bombs, one at a time, to a nearby quarry, detonated them.

The fact that the aircraft had its full bomb load on board at the time of the crash is puzzling. As mentioned earlier, the first consideration of the aircraft commander would have been to get his machine home safely and jettisoning the bombs would certainly have helped in this endeavour. There is a possibility that he may have still hoped to attack another target, though this seems unlikely and, of course, the release mechanism may have been damaged or faulty.

The crash happened at 1925 hours. Even allowing for British Summer Time, which may still have been in force, it would have been getting dark and the pilot may have been wiser to fly at a higher altitude in such a hilly region.

It is always interesting to envisage what lead up to events like these but here we are straying into the realms of conjecture. We do not know whether the aircraft was capable of flying higher or whether the pilot thought that he stood more chance of evading the defences by keeping low. The reasons for his actions will never be known for, at 7.25 pm on a cold October evening in 1940, they no longer had any relevance.

★   ★   ★

I decided to visit the site in late autumn. It had been a warm month, the warmest for 300 years they said. The coast road was fine and dry but, a few miles inland, rain began to fall and by the time I reached the road leading past Hafod Wen farm it had become a downpour. The farm buildings, quite a distance from the road, looked deserted while the gateway leading to the house was overgrown and so muddy I doubted the ability of my car to negotiate it.

Whilst sitting there wondering what to do next, a Honda quad, laden with hay, appeared through the gloom and sped past up the road. Peering through the misted rear window I saw it stop by a gate further up the road. Executing a quick 7-point turn, I raced up the road just in time to catch the driver. Clad from head to toe in waxed cotton, with just eyes and nose showing, the figure turned out to be the daughter of Gwilym Vaughan who moved into Hafod Wen shortly after the crash. She told me that the house was, indeed, unoccupied, that she had inherited the farm on the death of her father and that, if I cared to wait whilst she fed the cattle, she would point out the crash site to me.

There is a distinct depression in the ground, caused, no doubt, by the excavations of 1983. I decided to use my metal detector and soon brought to light a number of fragments, (not an easy task, as by now the rain was cascading down). It was with some relief that I took my leave, keeping just one small fragment to remind me of my visit to the spot where, some 54 years earlier, Heinz Havemann's desperate attempt to reach safety ended in tragedy.

MR 116/990600

Vickers Armstrong's Wellington Mk 1c DV800

The Welsh contribution to Bomber Command in air and ground crews is well known, what is not so familiar is its contribution in actual bomber aircraft.

The Vickers Armstrong's factory at Weybridge, Surrey, could not cope with the orders for the Wellington and, in any case, was vulnerable to air attack.

Another production line was set up at Squire's Gate near Blackpool and a further one at Broughton near Chester.

Breakdown of the production figures show that the Welsh factory was responsible for almost half:

```
WEYBRIDGE ......... 2515
SQUIRE'S GATE ..... 3406
BROUGHTON ........ 5540
                   11461
```

The last Wellington built left the Squire's Gate production line on October 13th, 1945.

One of those made at Broughton was a Mark 1c, R1333, which was paid for by contributions from V.A. employees. A Welsh dragon adorned its nose and a suitable ceremony took place on November 7th, 1940, when local dignitaries christened it with a bottle of champagne. (Or, as it was wartime, this may well have been some less notable liquid.)

Unfortunately, exactly one week later, on the 14th, the Luftwaffe took exception to Broughton's war effort and dropped some bombs on the airfield. There were no casualties but four aircraft were destroyed and a further 24 damaged. Thus, R1333 made and paid for by the VA workforce, never left the place of its birth, as it was one of those damaged beyond repair.

Thousands of Wellingtons did survive, however and these aircraft formed the equipment of many bomber squadrons and 25 OTUs during its service career. DV800, built at Broughton as one of a batch of 415 aircraft, was lost, complete with its entire crew, just 40 miles from its birthplace.

★　★　★

Official crash records of all aircraft (Form 1180) are available for study by researchers at the RAF Museum, Hendon. These give quite detailed information, although sometimes the location given is sketchy or inaccurate.

Study of the records for DV800 show that it was a Mark 1c, fitted with two Bristol Pegasus XVIII radial engines, numbers 240773 and 185390. This aircraft came from No. 27 OTU Lichfield, Staffordshire of No. 91 group Bomber Command.

The pilot was AUS 416004 Sgt E.H. Longbottom (RAAF) who had a total of 128 hours solo flying, 21 of which were on type, and 86 hours at night.

The aircraft took off on a cross-country exercise on the morning of July 19th, 1942. Cloud base at Lichfield was 1000 to 1500 feet, with tops above 7000 feet. The crew had been briefed to fly above cloud for the exercise and at 1230 the aircraft should have been over the sea, north of Llanfairfechan. Because of a navigational error, however, it was about 10 miles south of track. Official records can throw no light on the reason for the pilots decision to descend through the cloud, other than to suggest that the radio was unserviceable and that the pilot may have attempted to break cloud to obtain a pinpoint.

At 1206 hours the last radio message from DV800 was received. The cloud base over the Carneddau range at this time was about 2000 feet; the ridge between Carneddau Llywelyn and Dafydd, however, is considerably higher than that. The aircraft struck the ridge at about 2500 feet and burnt fiercely, killing all on board.

At the subsequent inquiry the C.O. stated that the crash was due to an error of navigation and thought that the radio must have been out of action.

The Air Officer Commanding stated that the pilot was contravening instructions in descending below 7000 feet.

Reading between the lines of the report, I gained the impression that an unfortunate combination of circumstances caused this tragedy. (A sad, but almost daily occurrence during this period of the war.)

R1333, paid for by VA employees, at the time of its christening.
Note the bottle of wine suspended by a string wrapped around the propeller.
Two oxygen bottles are tied to the fuselage to prevent the bottle damaging the fabric. After its destruction, R1333 was replaced by R1719, later lost on operations.

Wreckage from DV800 litter the mountainside.

A fragment of DV800 found on the mountainside. Brooklands Museum at Weybridge provided technical details from this drawing. It is part of the hydraulic bomb door mechanism. There were 12 on each side.

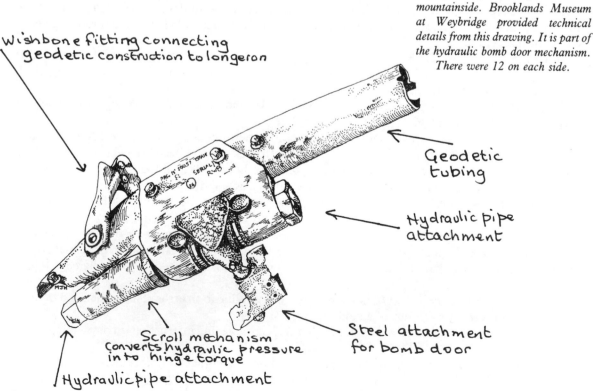

Wishbone fitting connecting geodetic construction to longeron

Geodetic tubing

Hydraulic pipe attachment

Scroll mechanism converts hydraulic pressure into hinge torque

Steel attachment for bomb door

Hydraulic pipe attachment

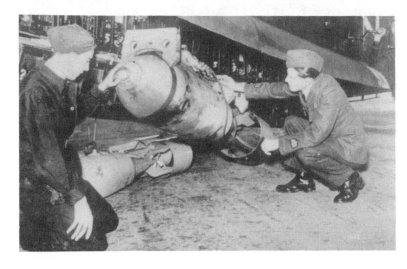

The part shown in the drawing can be seen just in front of the airman's forehead.

DV800 was the 17th Wellington of 27 OTU to be lost, three whilst on operations. One of those, DV934, also crashed on that same day, July 19th, whilst attempting an overshoot at Wellesbourne Mountford, near Stratford-on-Avon.

It is interesting to note that the official forms (F1180), raised before the aircraft was found, states "Aircraft missing". This was later crossed out and replaced with "Aircraft flew into hills", while an addition, after the Inquiry, states that it flew into "Mt Snowdon".

★   ★   ★

The journey to this site is best undertaken in combination with a visit to that of Lincoln RF511, as they are only about a quarter of a mile apart.

MR 115/675635

Avro Lancaster B Mk III NE132

The Lancaster has, together with the Spitfire, become the most well-known of wartime RAF aircraft. The fact that the Battle of Britain Memorial Flight still operates both these types at airshows throughout the country is a constant reminder of the debt we all owe to the crews that flew these aircraft.

There is one way, however, that the 'Lanc', as it was invariably known, differs from nearly all other long-serving wartime aircraft: the last of the 7,377 aircraft built was virtually the same as the first. True, the Mark II used Bristol Hercules radial engines but only 300 of these were built. The basic model was modified to carry certain loads, such as the 'bouncing bombs' used in the dams raid and the 12000 and 22000 lb Tallboy and Grand Slam bombs designed by Barnes Wallis. To all intents and purposes it was the case that they got it right first time and here I am ignoring its unfortunate progenitor, the Manchester.

Lancaster crew members were awarded 10 VCs during the war and in the thousands of Lancasters that failed to return must have been many unrecorded acts of supreme heroism.

★　★　★

Rolls-Royce could not keep pace with the demand for the Merlin engine and the Packard Motor Corp in America started a production line, eventually making over 60000 engines. These had a number of differences to the home produced item but was virtually the same engine.

The Lancaster Mark III differed from the Mark I mainly in the installation of the Packard built Merlin 28, (similar to the Merlin XX) of 1460 hp, giving it a maximum speed of 287 mph and a range of 1600 miles. NE132, the subject of this chapter, had one Merlin 28 in the port outer position, the remaining engines being Merlin 38s. These, equivalent to the British built Merlin 22, gave an extra 180 hp each. If the reader finds this difficult to follow, (as does the writer!) an interesting book on the subject★ is available from the Rolls-Royce Heritage Trust.

★　★　★

*A 4000 lb bomb about to be loaded
into a Lancaster.*

★ The Merlin in perspective — the combat years. By Alec Harvey-Bailey.

The twin peaks of the Rhinogydd.

*Left: Wreckage lies against
a mountain wall.*

In 1945, No. 1653 Heavy Conversion Unit was based at North Luffenham, in what was then Rutland. On February 6th, 1945, Fg. Off. D.H. Evans, an Australian, with six other crew members, took-off on a night navigation exercise, at approximately 2225 hours. He already had a total of 245 flying hours to his credit, 23 of them on Lancasters and 5 of those at night. It was a stormy night, with plenty of cumulonimbus storm cloud about. (CuNim produces extremely turbulent conditions, together with sudden drops in temperature. It can rip an aircraft apart and is avoided nowadays by using cloud and collision warning radar.)

Four hours into the flight, CuNim cloud was encountered and because of icing, turbulence, or a combination of the two the aircraft was thrown into a near vertical dive. The pilot struggled to regain control but in the process the tail section broke away and the aircraft crashed onto remote moorland in the foothills of the Rhinogydd, the tail section falling 3 miles away from the main wreckage. The aircraft disintegrated, caught fire and none of those on board had any chance of survival. The bodies of five of the crew members, Fg. Off. Moor, Sgt Neilson, Sgt Hodges, Sgt Sowden and Sgt Cliff were found by a party from RAF Llanbedr and sent by train to various destinations around Britain. The pilot, Fg. Off. Evans and another crew member were listed as 'missing'. This word, so awful for relatives to hear, meant that no sign of them could be found.

★   ★   ★

A study of the relevant accident report is revealing. The local inquiry suggested that the pilot lost control in cumulonimbus cloud and in pulling out of a dive, a break-up occurred. The squadron flying instructor was of the opinion that it may have been poor instrument flying. Further up the chain of command someone stated that the aircraft may have iced-up in cloud. The Air Investigation Branch (AIB) report stated that, flying in cloud, the pilot lost control, but the cause could not be determined, although icing was a possibility.

This last report ends with a most interesting statement, which I quote, " . . . unable to pull out of resultant steep dive, possibly because modifications to elevators not incorporated". This suggests that previous trouble in recovering from steep dives had been encountered and modifications to rectify this were in hand. It might be remembered that in the crash of Lancaster III JB471, on April 11th, 1944,* the aircraft also broke up whilst attempting to recover from a dive.

★   ★   ★

This is a comparatively easy site to reach but, because it is somewhat off the beaten track, only those interested in aviation archaeology are likely to find it. The Ordnance Survey Outdoor Leisure Map is the best bet here as it shows stone walls and tracks, making the search that much easier. It is an uphill walk but the site is only at about 1500 feet ASL; on the first part of the journey the twin peaks of Rhinog Fawr (2340 feet) and Rhinog Fach can be seen, with the prominent gap, Bwlch Drws Ardudwy, between them.

At the site, a shallow gorge is strewn with wreckage. I was told, beforehand, that the four engines remain and it does appear to be the case but the destruction is so complete that they have been shattered into a thousand pieces. Even taking into account that ATC units, collectors etc. have taken much away in the last 50 years there are still many recognisable engine parts to be seen.

Massive Merlin crankshafts lie broken and distorted in the heather, together with valves, oil pipes and masses of airframe fragments.

Standing on the desolate moor I could not help imagining the terror of that stormy February night, 50 years earlier, when Lancaster NE132 plunged down from the sky and realising that, mercifully, death for the crew must have been instantaneous.

MR 124/638288

* Down in Wales: Gwasg Carreg Gwalch 1994.

24 Squadron RAF and the Hudson
Lockheed Hudson Mk I N7253

Number 24 is the sixth most senior squadron in the RAF. Formed on September 1st, 1915 at Hounslow, it moved to France in the following February and became the first squadron to operate single seat fighters (the DH2 Scout) in combat.

The squadron's first Commanding Officer was Major L.J. Hawker VC DSO, who won great distinction both for himself and the squadron. He was later shot down and killed by the famous Baron von Richthofen. The squadron, however, exacted considerable revenge during the remainder of the war, by destroying no less than 297 enemy aircraft.

During the inter-war years, the squadron was engaged in communications duties, a role which it developed and continued during WW2. Many civil aircraft were impressed into service when the war began and a goodly number came to 24 sqn. As a result, it is estimated that the number of types used varies between 43 and 70! some of these only for a short period. One of those aircraft was the De Havilland Flamingo, operated by the King's Flight, which joined another already on the strength. The King's Flight then disbanded, 24 sqn being made responsible for all Royal flights, in addition to those of the Prime Minister, Winston Churchill.

One of the most important types operated by the squadron was the Lockheed Hudson. This American twin-engined aircraft was used almost exclusively in the coastal reconnaissance role at the outset of the war but, as they were supplemented by longer range aircraft more suitable for that task, additional Hudsons became available as transport aircraft.

Powered by 2 Wright Cyclone, 1,100 hp radial engines the Mark I had a maximum speed of 246 mph and an endurance of six hours. Over 2,000 Hudsons were delivered to the RAF, later versions, used exclusively as transports, having the mid-upper gun turret removed. (Back to the way it left the factory indeed, as the gun turret, made by Boulton and Paul, was fitted when the aircraft arrived in Britain.)

In April 1942, 24 squadron, in recognition of its 323 flights into besieged Malta in these unarmed aircraft, was accorded the great honour of delivering the George Cross medal awarded to the island by King George VI.

Perhaps, to give an idea of the type of flying carried out by the squadron during the war, we should look at the Operations Record Book for a typical day.

Place: Hendon. Day: July 17th, 1942.

0705: Flt Lt R.W. Reid takes-off in Dominie X7413 and has as his passenger, General Carl Spaatz (Commander of the USAAF 8th AF) who he flies to High Ercall and return.

0920: Flt Lt J.D. King, flying an Oxford air ambulance goes from Hendon to Northern Ireland and thence to Ringway, Manchester, with a stretcher case.

0940: Fg. Off. P. Loat conveys a number of senior officers to Squires Gate and Liverpool in another Dominie.

1015: Using Dominie X7413 on its second flight of the day, W/O D. Brown takes two senior officers to Gosport and Warmwell before returning to Hendon.

1030: Flt Lt B. Rogers takes off in Hudson N7253 for Northern Ireland.

1220: Sqn Ldr R.M. Blennerhassett flying Hudson FH460 departs en route for Gibraltar with 1700 lbs of freight and one passenger. After one abortive attempt, he leaves Gibraltar on July 22nd with 2003 lbs of freight for Malta, then returning to Gibraltar. He leaves again on the 27th with a further 1795 lbs of vital supplies for Malta before going back to Gibraltar with 4 passengers and mail eventually returns to Hendon on July 29th.

1305: Flt Lt C.H. Willis, flying D H Flamingo R2766 (ex Kings Flight) takes Mr and Mrs Winant (a senior American diplomat) to Chivenor, returning empty the next day.

The above is only a list of departures; many aircraft were away from base ferrying vital war material and personnel, particularly to Malta. Indeed, on one single day earlier in 1942, at the height of the Battle of Malta, there were no less than 13 Hudsons en route from Gibraltar, three of which were lost.

* * *

FOUR TYPES USED BY 24 SQUADRON

A Fairey 111F with the squadron emblem, a black and red chevron, on the tail.

Curtiss Cleveland.

De Havilland Flamingo, RAF serial number R2766 ex Kings Flight, still bearing its civil markings.

Avro York.

In these accounts I usually give a much shortened version of the official records but here, for the interest of the reader, I quote at length.

On July 17th, 1942 the scheduled flight to N. Ireland left at 1030 am. Hudson N7253 was crewed by:

Flt Lt J.B. Rogers, Pilot
F. Sgt T.D. Butcher, Navigator
Sgt C.R. Bell, W/Operator
AC, K.M. Tucker, Ground Engineer

After an uneventful flight to Sydenham airport the aircraft commenced its return journey with the following passengers:

Sqn Ldr A. Hoggar, Wg Cdr M. McMillan, Flt Lt B. Bannister, Plt Off. N. Kearney, Lt Cdr A. Waring, Major Watt, Mr E. Armitage, Mr H. Smith and Mr C. Coatman.

★ ★ ★

Circumstances of the Accident

The accident occurred in the course of a scheduled mail flight between Belfast and Hendon. The outward trip had been made on the same morning and apart from an overheard conversation between the wireless operator and the observer to the effect that static interference with the radio equipment had been experienced no untoward incident was reported on arrival. The aircraft took off from Sydenham for the return journey with a crew of 4 and 9 passengers; 146 lbs of mail were carried. It left at 1400 hrs and a sound plot obtained by the Royal Observer Corps indicated that an aircraft crossed the Welsh coast at Rhyl about ¾ hour later at an estimated height of 6,000 ft. A few minutes after that the aeroplane was heard over the village of Llanfair D.C. about 18 miles S.E. of Rhyl. The evidence of witnesses as to subsequent events was very contradictory and therefore not reliable but sounds were heard as if the aircraft was performing aerobatics in the clouds. Shortly after this it was observed spinning from low cloud followed by a detached wing. One witness stated that she saw a ball of fire like a "flash of orange flame" before the aircraft came into view. It burst into flames on impact and was completely demolished. All the passengers and crew had remained in the aircraft and were killed instantly.

The weather at the time was bad with low cloud and heavy rain.

Lockheed Hudson transports
in the Middle East.

Further Particulars

(a) The airframe was constructed by the Lockheed Aircraft Corporation and reassembled in this country at Speke. Its flight trials were completed in July 1939 and it was first delivered to the Service in that month. It was delivered to Cunliffe-Owen Aircraft Ltd in April 1941 for general servicing and a major inspection and was allotted to No. 24 (C) squadron in August on completion of the work. That squadron completed a major inspection on 29.6.42. A daily inspection was carried out on the morning of the day of the accident. The airframe had done about 385 hours flying and the engines had a running time of 183 and 327 hours for port and starboard respectively.

For the flight in question the aircraft was loaded to within about 200 lb of the allowable all-up weight.

On 17.3.42 while the aircraft was on a similar flight it was struck by lightning while flying near Lydney. Following a loud explosion and a flash behind the port wing the cabin filled with smoke and it was discovered that the trailing aerial was burned off about 3 ft from the splice and that the reel had broken away from its mounting. Damage to the aircraft was confined to the radio equipment and the flight was completed without further incident.

Flight Lieutenant Rogers began flying as a Service pilot in April 1940 but it is understood that he had considerable previous experience as a commercial pilot. He joined No. 24(C) squadron in November 1941. His total service flying, covering 23 different types, amounted to 1350 hours including 25 hours as first pilot and 11 hours as second pilot in Hudsons. The total amount of instrument flying recorded in his log book was 7½ hours as pilot.

Weather conditions locally at the time of the accident were poor with low cloud covering the hills. Heavy rain was falling and the visibility was 10 furlongs.

Another Hudson from the same squadron en route from Jurby to Hendon crossed the Welsh coast at Colwyn Bay about 1 hour after the accident. It had climbed to about 10,000 ft having broken cloud at about 9,000 ft but ran into a bank of cumulus at 10-11,000 ft over the coast. It remained in cloud at 11,000 ft as far as Worcester and then lost height to 2-3,000 ft over the Chilterns. At 11,000 ft no icing or static was encountered as the pilot put it "to cause any difficulties to a pilot of Flight Lieutenant Rogers' calibre". Very bumpy conditions were experienced at the lower levels.

The crash occurred in a field near Llanfair Dyffryn Clwyd about 18 miles S.E. of Rhyl and 2¾ miles west of track between Rhyl and Worcester.

The aircraft had struck the ground at fairly high speed in a steep dive and in the inverted position. Apart from a few scattered components the wreckage was fairly compact and had therefore suffered severe damage from fire which broke out on impact. The entire fuselage, centre section and engine installations were gutted, the former being reduced to ash. The starboard wing was thrown to one side and came to rest standing on its leading edge a few yards from the main fire area. The inner end of this wing in the region of the attachment to the centre section had melted and the whole of the bottom surface was badly scorched. None of the fuselage or wing parts which had been thrown clear of the main wreckage showed any signs of fire damage. The port wing which had become detached in the air was found 400 yards SE of the main wreckage and a section of flap adjacent to the wing fracture with a portion of top wing skin came to earth 300 yds further on.

Conclusions

The wing had been struck by a single stroke of lightning of moderate intensity having a succession of approximately equally spaced current peaks, but it is not considered that any appreciable structural damage to the plane or electrical injury to the pilot would have occurred.

It is possible, however, that the pilot was momentarily blinded by the flash and he might also have been injured by the blast of air from the flash or by being struck by damaged parts of the machine, such as broken windows due to the air blast. Alternatively, these broken parts might jam the controls.

Apart from the damaged wing tip and the possible detachment of the trailing aerial there was no evidence in any of the components not destroyed by fire to suggest that major structural damage had been caused by the discharge.

Observations

In the appendix to the report brief details are given of some recorded cases of aircraft being struck by lightning where either structural damage, radio defects or loss of control have ensued. It will be seen from the report and the appendix that two Hudson aircraft (both from No. 24(C) squadron) have each been struck on two occasions. The Commanding Officer of the Squadron, although admitting that his aircraft do a considerable amount of bad weather flying has expressed concern at the apparent proneness of the Hudson to being struck by lightning and suggested an investigation by the R.A.E. with a view to taking any possible preventive action. The squadron operates numerous different types, wood and metal construction, and in only one instance has a type other than a Hudson been struck. This was a Dominie.

Many years after the crash a house, Erw Fair, was built on the site and, whilst excavating prior to laying the foundations, an amount of molten alloy was found. One large piece remains there still.

Despite a protracted metal detector search of the field next to the house, no other sign of wreckage remains.

★ ★ ★

24 squadron operates Lockheed aircraft to this day; The Hercules.

MR 116/133550

Republic P-47D Thunderbolt 42-75090

The winter of 1943/4 saw the Allied bomber offensive gaining momentum by day and night. It also saw the German fighter force at its most effective. During the period November 1943 to March 1944 RAF Bomber Command lost its entire front line strength of over 800 aircraft.

In daylight, the USAAF was faring little better. On September 27th, 1943 during an attack by 291 B-17 Flying Fortresses on the ball-bearing factories at Schweinfurt, sixty aircraft were lost.

The beginning of 1944 was to provide little relief for the bomber crews. The P-51 Mustang, which later was to provide escort for the bombers all the way to the target, was not yet available in sufficient numbers.

After the P-47 Thunderbolts reached the limit of their endurance, the bombers were on their own.

January 11th, 1944 saw the 182nd bombing mission undertaken by the 8th Air Force. A double pronged attack was planned; 177 B17s were detailed to bomb Oschersleben and a further 114 were to attack Halberstadt. Escort for these missions was provided by 177 Thunderbolts operating mainly at low level and 44 P-51 Mustangs.

After the majority of the fighter escort had turned back, the Oschersleben raid ran into stiff opposition and 34 of the B-17s failed to return. With a further 8 lost on the Halberstadt attack this was the biggest loss since the ill fated Schweinfurt mission.*

The B-17 crews claimed 3 enemy fighters destroyed and the escorting P-47s another three. (During this operation Col. James H. Howard won the Medal of Honor (US equivalent of the VC) for his outstanding bravery whilst leading the Low Protection Wing).

Only two P-47s failed to return to their bases; both crashed in Britain.

★ ★ ★

1st Lt William N. Tucker had flow over 250 hours since qualifying as a pilot on March 20th, 1943, four of these on instruments. His last instrument rating was in June of that year. He was based at East Wretham in Norfolk with the 370th Fighter Squadron. He flew P-47 serial number 42-75090. (It is not unlikely that this aircraft was allocated to him because of its similarity to his own service number, 0-675890).

On January 11th, 1944 he was detailed to fly as part of the B-17 escort force. On their return, they ran into bad weather and whilst flying on instruments Lt Tucker became separated from the rest of his squadron. Finding no gaps in the cloud, he continued westwards until it became obvious that he had overshot his base by a considerable margin. He turned onto a reciprocal heading and began to lose height slightly in the hope of fixing his position. Unbeknown to him, he had strayed further west than he had thought and in the descent, clipped the 1100 foot top of Moel Bentyrch near Llanfair Caereinion. The aircraft careered down the steep eastern side of the hill disintegrating as it did so.

When Milton Jones, the local doctor, arrived on the scene the pilot was still alive in the wreckage but died whilst the doctor was treating him.

A P-47 being towed through the streets of Liverpool to be assembled at Speke.

* Approx. 4100 B-17s were lost in action over Europe in WW2.

Moel Bentyrch. 42-75090 struck the summit from the west (left), the wreckage crashing down the steep eastern side.

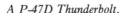
A P-47D Thunderbolt.

At the subsequent inquiry, Lt R.B. Platt, the Staff Weather Officer certified that the ceiling at the time was 1000 feet with 8 tenths cloud in moderate continuous rain.

★   ★   ★

42-75090 was built at the Republic factory at Farmingdale N.Y. on September 6th, 1943. On the following day 42-75101 left the same factory. Of some 15,000 Thunderbolts made during the war, these two aircraft had their final resting places just 11 miles apart when, on May 4th, 1944 Lt John W. Beauchamp of the 495 FTG crashed on Mynydd Copog and was killed.

★   ★   ★

Moel Bentyrch, though only just over 1000 feet high is a prominent feature to the north of the Welshpool-Dolgellau road, Gelli farmhouse lies in its shadow.

After gaining permission to park the car, I followed the footpath that runs around the base of the hill. Though the western side of Moel Bentyrch climbs gradually to the summit, the eastern face drops sharply with rocky crags, petering out into scree and mossy, slippery grass. This is the face that 42-75090 careered down; indeed not many years ago, an engine cylinder was found embedded in the wall at the bottom of the hill.

Fragments can still be found in the scree and the owner of Gelli showed me two quite large pieces, painted grey, that he had found in a nearby field.

MR 125/055095

Vickers-Armstrong's Supermarine Spitfire Mk 11A P7979

The Spitfire was designed by R.J. Mitchell. Born in 1895, he joined Pemberton Billing Ltd at the Supermarine works Southampton in 1916 as a draughtsman, soon becoming an integral part of the design team. Supermarine specialised in marine aircraft, as indeed their name implies, and did not concern themselves with single seat fighters.

In 1913 Jacques Schneider, believing that the future of aviation lay in flying boats and seaplanes, offered a trophy, competition for which, he hoped would advance their development.

In 1923, however, the Americans entered the contest with what were little more than racing seaplanes. These outclassed their flying boat rivals by a considerable margin.

R.J. Mitchell then designed a series of high performance seaplanes based on Rolls-Royce engines. The last of this series, the S6B, won the trophy outright for Britain in 1931. (It now resides in the RAF Museum, Hendon.) Two weeks later, Flt Lt Stainforth set up a World Speed Record of 407.5 mph, in an S6B serial number S1595.

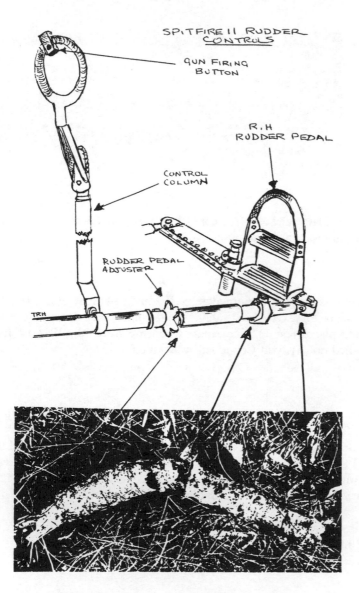

SPITFIRE II RUDDER CONTROLS

GUN FIRING BUTTON

R.H RUDDER PEDAL

CONTROL COLUMN

RUDDER PEDAL ADJUSTER

TRH

What at first sight appears to be an old rusty pipe, turns out to be, on closer inspection, part of the rudder assembly of Spitfire P7979.

*Supermarine S6B S1596
which took the world speed record
on September 13th, 1931.*

*A Supermarine Spitfire.
This is a Mk Vb.*

*Left: Sydney Pritchard.
P7979 crashed in the field behind
him and the only fragments found
were only a few feet to his right.*

The development of the Spitfire stemmed directly from the Schneider Trophy seaplanes. The Spitfire made its first flight on March 5th, 1936 and the rest, as the saying goes, is history.

In June 1937 R.J. Mitchell died, thus never witnessing the effect his design would have on the course of that history.

★   ★   ★

The Spitfire Mark 11A was powered by a Rolls-Royce Merlin XII of 1175 hp, giving it a speed of 357 mph, but by 1944 had long been replaced in front-line squadrons by later marks. (Indeed, by January 1944 the Mark XIV was entering service.) The earlier marks, however, continued to be used by OTUs for training purposes.

Spitfire 11A P7979 was one of a batch of 1000 aircraft built under contract number 98/687/39, at the vast factory at Castle Bromwich. It was delivered to the RAF on January 4th, 1941 and served with 54, 602, 545, 411, 121 and 340 squadrons. Damaged whilst on operations, it was repaired by Scottish Aviation Ltd, Prestwick and then allocated to 61 OTU Rednal, Shropshire.

* * *

Fg. Off. John Worth Wright (25) of the RCAF was trained at No. 20 Elementary Flying Training School in Canada, passing out as a pilot of 'average' ability. By the time he was posted to B Flight No. 61 OTU he had accrued 662 flying hours and up to the time of the accident a further 7 on the Spitfire.

On February 5th, 1944 B Flight Commander Flt Lt K.A. Mason, authorised Fg. Off. Wright to carry out a height climb to 30,000 feet spinning practice from 20,000 feet to 12,000 feet followed by aerobatics. This was the pilot's first height climb with oxygen at Rednal although his log book showed high altitude flying in Canada including one up to 30000 feet.

Whilst at 61 OTU he had been through the decompression chamber and had received instruction on the Spitfire oxygen system. Flt Lt Mason authorised four other similar flights to take place as soon as the aircraft had been refuelled from previous sorties. Because of cumulative delays in the flying programme Fg. Off. Wright in Spitfire P7979 finally took off at 17.25 hours, about 25 minutes later than had been originally intended. At 17.40 hours he made a transmission asking for a 'fix' giving his height as 20,000 feet. At about 17.55 the aircraft crashed vertically at high speed under engine power into a field at Bryn Farm, Berriew, near Newtown. The pilot was killed instantly. The subsequent Court of Inquiry headed by Wg. Cdr. C.H. Schofield (A.D. GB.*) concluded that as the entire aircraft wreckage was so deeply buried and disintegrated, no control settings could be determined, nor could the oxygen system yield any useful evidence. However, it was clear that the aircraft was not spinning at the time of impact and the most likely cause was that the pilot lost consciousness through lack of oxygen.

* * *

Mr Sydney Pritchard was in the barn at Bryn farm on a snowy February afternoon, preparing feed for the cattle, when he heard an aircraft roaring down, 'as if in a power dive'. There followed a terrific explosion and, looking out of the barn, he saw a column of smoke and small pieces of smoking debris raining down from the sky. The aircraft had buried itself into the ground just a hundred yards or so from the barn, with the shattered wings on each side of the crater, the only recognisable piece, he said, was the tailwheel. Mr Pritchard telephoned the police, but by the time the RAF team of about 7 men arrived (probably from Rednal) it was getting dark. They set up their tent in the field, and sifted through the wreckage. As far as Mr Pritchard could see, nothing could be found of the pilot's remains.

Next day a number of sightseers arrived at the site and, according to Sydney Pritchard, the RAF men gave them " . . . guided tours of the site". Soon after, the RAF personnel left and were replaced by an Army unit who fenced off the area and would not allow anyone near. Lifting tackle was brought to the scene but the engine, deep in the muddy ground, could not be extracted, so the crater was filled in.

A few years ago a group came to the site in an attempt to salvage the engine but, after many hours and reaching a depth of about 10 feet, gave up the struggle. A Rolls-Royce Merlin XII, may therefore lie buried under this field somewhere.

* * *

* In November 1943 Fighter Command as such had been disbanded, replaced by the 2nd Tactical Air Force and Air Defence of Great Britain.

Mr Pritchard walked with me the short distance to the site but, despite scanning the ground with a metal detector for an hour or so, no sign of wreckage was found.

Later, as about to return to my car, disappointed, I photographed Mr Pritchard leaning on his garden fence, just a few yards from the crash site. As an afterthought, I said that I would look at the tiny strip of grass alongside the house and almost immediately found number of pieces: a sizable panel painted dark grey showing it to be from the upper camouflaged surface of the aircraft, a segment of a main wheel and, on the smallest fragment of all a serial number prefixed by '300' as used for the Spitfire.

MR 136/166023

Bryn farm. P7979 crashed in the foreground. Mr Pritchard was in the barn on the right at the time of the crash.

Vickers-Armstrong's Wellington Mk III X3785

There was nothing intrinsically wrong with the Bristol Pegasus engine. Indeed, this fine motor served the RAF well in such famous aircraft as the Hampden and the Sunderland. It was in the Wellington, however, that it was most widely used, every one of its 1000 horses (each engine) needed to propel some 14 tons of aeroplane and payload. Thus, when an engine failed, crews were in an unenviable position, frequently ending in disaster.

In the Mark II Wellington, Rolls-Royce Merlins were used. These proved an improvement but Merlins, needed for the Spitfire, Lancaster and Mosquito were in short supply. With the Mark III, the Bristol Hercules of 1500 hp went a long way to improving the situation, giving greater speed, range and, above all, better reliability.

Just the same, no engine is perfect. The Pegasus, like most piston engines utilised "poppet" valves, much the same as those fitted in your car today. The Hercules used sleeve valves, which might, simply be described as cylinder liners rotating to cover and uncover intake and exhaust ports. It was a fault in this mechanism which was the main factor in the loss of X3785.

This aircraft was built at Squire's Gate, Blackpool, as one of a batch of 500 machines.

* * *

By 1943, after the introduction of four-engined aircraft into Bomber Command, the Mark III Wellington became available to OTUs for training purposes. (Much to the relief of the instructors, no doubt.)

No. 27 OTU, at Lichfield, had a number of Mark IIIs on strength. On the night of May 14/15th, 1943 Fg. Off. J.N. Roff, a pupil pilot, together with six other crew members were detailed for a night flying exercise. Although a "pupil", Roff had 301 hours in his log book; 29 on Wellingtons, 10 of which were at night.

It was a clear moonlit night when they lifted-off from the runway at Lichfield at precisely 2250 hours. Some three and a half hours later, the sleeve drive on one of the engines failed and it caught fire. The blaze being uncontrollable, and the aircraft becoming too low for the crew to bale out, crashed on a hillside just 250 yards north of Lake Vyrnwy. It exploded on impact, killing all those on board.

* * *

Lake Vyrnwy, or Llyn Efyrnwy to give its correct Welsh name, is not a natural lake. The scheme to make what was called, "A bare and featureless valley" into a lake was begun in 1881, by damming the Afon Efyrnwy.

The water thus stored, estimated at the time to be some 12,000,000 gallons, was to be supplied to the Liverpool Corporation. The largest lake of its kind in Wales, it is five miles long and nearly a mile across and, apart from the rather quaint Victorian towers, looks entirely natural. Lake Vyrnwy provides excellent fishing and although somewhat off the beaten track, is a magnet for tourists.

* * *

The crash site is now covered by woodland but this is not dense and the area is littered with small fragments, including tiny pieces of engine cooling fins.

MR 125/006211

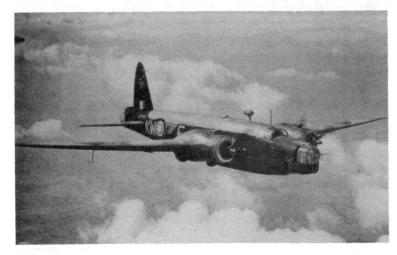

Wellington III X3763 was on the same production line at Squire's Gate as X3785 and belonged to 425 squadron RCAF. It failed to return from Stuttgart on April 15th, 1942.

Lake Vyrnwy: the crash site is off the picture to the left.

North American Mustang III FX898

Although produced to meet a British requirement (as mentioned elsewhere in this volume) of the 14000 or so Mustangs manufactured during WW2, only 2600 served with the RAF. They were used mainly in the Army Co-operation role; low-level reconnaissance, including photography and attacking targets of opportunity such as railways, and road transport etc. These operations were carried out at hedge-hopping height and were extremely vulnerable to ground fire. This was compounded by the fact that the Mustang, at the time a comparative rarity, was often mistaken for the Messerschmitt Bf109 and many were lost as a consequence of so called 'friendly fire'!

The first operation was undertaken on May 10th, 1942, by Fg. Off. G. Dawson, in Mustang I AG418.

The Mustang III was the first version to use the Merlin engine and was similar to the American P-51C. Using the Packard built V-1650-7 engine, it could attain a maximum speed of 442 mph and was armed with four 0.5 inch machine guns, together with a bomb load of 1000 lbs.

While continuing the low level work of its Allison engined predecessor, the Mustang III provided escorts for Bomber Command when it began daylight operations in the latter stages of the war.

The Mustang was also effective in countering the flying bombs being launched against Southern England, shooting down 233 "doodle bugs", as they were known.

A formation of RAF Mustang IIIs.

Fragments of FX898 lie amongst the rocks.

The Rolls-Royce Merlin installed in a Mustang III.

The CO of No. 315 (Polish) squadron RAF, Wing Commander E. Horbazewski, on seeing one of his pilots crash land his Mustang in France, landed in a nearby field, ran across to free the pilot from the wreckage and then flew home with him on his lap! Wg. Cdr. Horbazewski shot down 16 enemy aircraft and four flying bombs, before being killed in action.

★   ★   ★

Because so many airworthy Mustangs still survive, there is great interest in them and their wartime activities with the USAAF. However, the sacrifice of the gallant RAF Mustang pilots, many of them Polish, operating in the hazardous ground attack role, should not be forgotten.★

★   ★   ★

★ On a lighter note, the author's pilot whilst flying on airdrop trials, was, during the war, a 2nd Tactical Air Force pilot, flying Mustangs. He related how, whilst at low-level over the Rhine, he flew over a collapsed bridge, not noticing that the cables which had supported it were still strung out across the river. One of them took off a wing tip and, on return to base, he was hauled in front of the unamused squadron commander. Luckily, the aircraft was due to be returned to the UK for replacement and no further action was taken.

Flying Officer A.J. McArthy, an Australian, was on the staff of 61 OTU, 12 Group Fighter Command, Rednal, Shropshsire. He had accrued 245 flying hours, 46 of them on Mustangs. (If this doesn't seem too many, it should be remembered that a fighter sortie might be less than an hour in duration.)

The German surrender was signed on May 4th, 1945. The next day, at 0920, Fg. Off. McArthy, took off on a training flight. He was briefed to fly VFR* i.e. not in cloud and only in the local area.

The flight proceeded uneventfully for over an hour before the aircraft encountered low cloud. Fg. Off. McArthy radioed base for a "fix" and was given a vector** of 160 degrees, which would have taken him back to Rednal, some 20 miles away. This was, however, later transmitted as "350 degrees" and he took up this heading, switching to another radio channel for radar guidance. On realising their error, Air Traffic Control at Rednal transmitted the correct heading, telling him to climb immediately. By this time, however, the pilot was on a different radio channel and did not receive the message.

At 1033 hours FX898 clipped the eastern ridge of Minera mountain and crashed into the heather covered hillside, killing the pilot. A few feet higher and he would have survived this unfortunate accident, the result, as is so often the case, of a combination of errors on the part of pilot and ground control.

The subsequent court of inquiry decided that the pilot was contravening instructions by flying in cloud. It was concluded that, if the pilot had been in sight of the ground, he would have realised that he had been given a reciprocal bearing. (This was, presumably, proof that he was indeed in cloud, contrary to instructions.) Nevertheless the Air Officer Commanding ordered a further Inquiry into the organisation of Rednal Flying Control.

*　*　*

The best way to approach the site is from a point on the Horseshoe Pass road at approximately MR 117/232484. A path to the east leads up through the heather but after a short while you must stride (or stumble) off in a more southerly direction.

Wreckage is to be found in a number of places in small holes, easily overlooked. A piece I picked up, turned out to be part of the Packard engine cooling system, much other wreckage has no doubt sunk into the peaty ground and been covered by heather.

MR 117/243463

* Visual Flight Rules
** Course to steer

Avro Anson Mk 1 N5019

Although 11,020 Ansons were built, comparatively few were engaged in active operations during the war. It was an Anson which made the first RAF attack on a U-boat. On one unusual occasion in June 1940, three Ansons were attacked by *nine* BF109s and managed to shoot down two of the German fighters, damaging others. Nevertheless it was as a training aircraft that the Anson made its mark.

In 1939, with many Ansons already in service, an order for 1500 training versions was placed and large numbers were also produced in Canada for the Commonwealth Air Training Plan.

Powered by two Armstrong-Siddeley 'Cheetah' radial engines of 350 hp each it had a maximum speed of 188 mph. The fuselage was of metal framing, covered with fabric, whilst the wings of earlier models were constructed of wood. (Accounting for the large number of brass woodscrews found at Anson crash sites.)

The Anson first flew at Woodford on March 24th 1935 and the last example, a T Mk 21 WJ 561, left the production line in May 1952.

How many of these trainers were lost is probably recorded somewhere but, at a guess, must run into many hundreds.

This was no reflection on the aircraft, known in the Service as "Faithful Annie", but rather on the duties it was called upon to perform. These involved pilot, but more particularly navigator training, with a minimum of navigational aids and weather information, crews often believed themselves to be in a different location that was actually the case. N5019 was one of these.

★　★　★

On July 9th 1940 at 15 OTU Harwell, Berkshire, with a crew of 4, Sgt A.C. Smith was briefed for a night-flying detail.

They took-off as planned and, at about 2220 hrs, were flying over the Welsh Marches. The Observer (an aircrew grade later re-named Navigator) believed that they were still over England and could come down safely through the cloud. The pilot began his descent but at about 2230, N5019 struck the northern slopes of Y Gamrhiw near Llanwrthwl. Four of the crew were killed instantly, but the pilot, though severely injured, survived.

For most of the night he stumbled down the steep heather-covered slopes, until, just about at the end of his tether, he reached Ty Coch farm. The farmer Mr Pugh, made him as comfortable as he could and called an ambulance. The ambulance from Builth Wells arrived, driven by Mr H.L. Weale, who said that they had to carry Sgt Smith quite a way up the track, as the ambulance could not get to the farm buildings.

Sgt Smith was taken to Builth Wells Cottage Hospital and eventually made a full recovery before returning to his duties. He was later posted to 97 squadron and on November 24th 1941 was killed when the Avro Manchester bomber he was flying was involved with Hurricane V6864, in a collision over Sutton Bridge airfield.

★　★　★

A pre-war photograph of one of the first Ansons to be delivered to Australia (L9163).

The last mark of Anson, the T21.

The reader will have to show little skill in map reading to find the location, although he will need sharp eyes if he is to avoid walking past it without noticing. Only small wreckage scattered in the heather, is to be seen.

The view from the ridge of Y Gamrhiw is superb.

Just as aircraft these days do a "beacon crawl" going from one radio beacon to the next, this is a "cairn crawl" where you can usually keep two cairns in sight to navigate by.

MR 147/943616

ACKNOWLEDGEMENTS

The author wishes to extend his gratitude to the following individuals and organisations that gave such invaluable assistance in the writing of this book.

The Air Historical Branch, Alfred Brown, Bundesarchiv, Canadian Defence Force, Clwyd Record Office, John Davies, Mervyn Davies, Katherine Davies, Forest Enterprise, Geoff Hill, Doreen Hill, Imperial War Museum, Don James, Mark Jones, R.E. Jones, David Jones, Matthew Rimmer, Len Roberts, Rachel Stewart, The RAF Museum (especially Anna McIlwaine of the Research Department), and to Shirley Evans without whom it would have been impossible.

★　★　★

Bibliography

Aircraft of the Royal Air Force since, 1918, O. Thetford, Putnam.
British Military Aircraft Serials, B. Robertson, Ian Allan.
*Fallen Eagles,*E. Doylerush, Midland Counties.
The Handley Page Halifax, K. Merrick, Aston.
Luftwaffe Handbook, A. Price, Ian Allen.
No Moon Tonight, D. Charlwood, Goodall.
Spitfire. The History, Morgan & Shacklady, Guild.
The Merlin in Perspective — The Combat Years, A Harvey-Bailey, R.R. Heritage Trust.

Aviation in Wales

Early Aviation in North Wales *168pp. £2.75. 0-86381-119-1.*
This book sets out to chronicle the history of aviation in North Wales from the time of early nineteenth century balloon flights to the outbreak of World War II in 1939.
Roy Sloan

Wings of War over Gwynedd
Aviation in Gwynedd during World War II *200pp. £4.50. 0-86381-189-2. Many maps & illustrations.*
This book traces the history of aviation in Gwynedd during the momentous years of the Second World War — a period of rapid and dramatic development.
Readable, well researched and illustrated with seventy photographs, the book provides a fascinating view of wartime aviation in Gwynedd and as such ranks as a major contribution to the history of aviation in Wales.
Roy Sloan

Aircraft Crashes
Flying accidents in Gwynedd 1910-1990 *168pp. £5.50. 0-86381-281-3. Many photographs.*
The sixteen stories which make up this book have been chosen in order to provide a broad view of the types of flying accidents which have taken place within the geographical boundaries of Gwynedd. The region's mountains are the highest in England and Wales and, not surprisingly, present a natural hazard themselves.
Roy Sloan

Down in Wales
Visits to some war-time air crash sites *94pp. £6.50. 0-86381-283-X. Many maps & illustrations.*
This comprehensive volume on wartime air crash sites will no doubt prove invaluable to aircraft enthusiasts. All the sites were visited and researched in the three years prior to publication and therefore it contains much information, not available elsewhere, about the current state of these sites.
Terence R. Hill

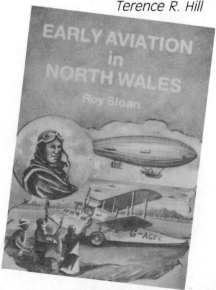